no more
clutter

SUE KAY

no more
clutter

how to clear your space
and free your life

HODDER

First published in Great Britain in 2005 by Hodder and Stoughton
A division of Hodder Headline
This paperback edition published in 2006

A Hodder paperback

6

A CIP catalogue record for this title
is available from the British Library

ISBN 978 0 340 83677 4

Typeset in Sabon by Hewer Text UK Ltd, Edinburgh
Printed and bound in the UK by CPI Mackays, Chatham ME5 8TD

Hodder Headline's policy is to use papers that are natural,
renewable and recyclable products and made from wood grown
in sustainable forests. The logging and manufacturing processes
are expected to conform to the environmental regulations
of the country of origin

Hodder and Stoughton Ltd
A division of Hodder Headline
338 Euston Road
London NW 1 3BH

Acknowledgements

Firstly I would like to thank all my clients whose struggles and successes have inspired this book. Their courage and trust in opening their homes and lives to me have been immense.

Heartfelt thanks to those who encouraged me along the way: Alison Rice from Speakeasy, Catherine Riney and Matt Garner from CENTA, and of course my ever-supportive husband Nick.

Not forgetting Rosie Bennett who even at 11 had plenty to teach me about catchy headings and smart shopping.

Last but not least, I would like to express my gratitude to Liz Puttick from the Puttick Literary Agency who believed in the book from the outset. Special thanks to Rowena Webb and the team at Hodder Mobius, particularly to Helen Coyle for her guidance and invaluable insights.

To Nick, who has always treasured me

Contents

introduction

Clutter and Life in 21st-Century Britain

Our homes are sanctuaries, places to relax, socialise and bring up our families in, as well as, increasingly, places to work from. We live in a time when there is constant media emphasis on having a beautiful and stylish home. Yet many people feel their homes have been taken over by possessions. Life in Britain today has become busier and more stressful. As we endlessly buy and acquire more and more stuff, it is now commonplace to feel overwhelmed by clutter.

It is a myth that being organised is a natural talent that you are born with. Decluttering and getting organised are skills you can learn. This book will give you both the emotional insights and the practical tools you need to achieve a clutter-free home. By letting go of clutter, you will regain pleasure in your home and the things you own. Crucially, you will attain a sense of being in control rather than controlled by your possessions.

SO WHAT IS CLUTTER?

Clutter is things you no longer use or love. It's too much stuff and furniture for the space you live in. It's disorganised things like unfiled paperwork. It's broken electrical equipment. It's clothes that are two sizes too big or make you feel frumpy. It's junk in the loft. It's books you'll never read again. It's useless things like old keys you keep just in case. It's unwanted presents you feel too guilty to give away. It's cards and photos that remind you of unhappy times in your life. It's unfinished projects like the button you've been meaning to sew on for months or the mound of unsorted photos shoved into the bottom of your wardrobe.

You know it is clutter because it irritates and upsets you. You find yourself avoiding areas of your home because you can't face thinking about them. Clutter causes stagnation, so you feel as though you are standing still in your life. Your dreams of moving home or starting a new business are put on hold until you feel more on top of things.

Living with clutter can cause enormous stress. People at the end of their tether fantasise about a natural disaster sweeping away all their possessions. No wonder they daydream about downshifting, living in a cabin in the woods and leaving all their stuff behind. They remember with nostalgia a time in their lives when they could pack all their possessions into the boot of the car.

WHAT EXACTLY IS DECLUTTERING?

Decluttering is a much more profound experience than just tidying up. It is making choices about what things we keep and what we let go of. In the world today there are many things we can't control. But we can take charge of what we have in our homes.

Decluttering is a kind of stock-taking. When you are cluttered you lose touch with what you actually own. The first step is to rediscover your possessions. As you streamline your things, you reconnect with what you have and where it is stored in your home. You let go of stuff that you no longer need, use or love. You keep the 'edited highlights' of your life, like your favourite photos, and let go of all the out-of-focus ones. Your reward is a home that feels fantastic, organised and relaxing.

MY DECLUTTERING JOURNEY

I am writing this book because I passionately believe that letting go of clutter is a life-changing experience. Radically decluttering my home was a turning point in my life and I've never looked back. In my 30s I was restless, feeling bogged down and looking for a new direction. When I looked around my home I felt oppressed, as though I was living in a museum of my past.

Since my teens I had spent weekends rooting around jumble sales and second-hand shops in true magpie fashion. I loved kitsch and vintage finds. I collected snowstorms from around the globe and glitzy jewellery I picked up at Camden Market. My home was cluttered with numerous books, clothes I no longer wore, paintings I was sick of looking at and boxes of sentimental memorabilia.

I woke up one morning when my husband was in America and suddenly I knew it was time to let go of all the stuff that was holding me back. I wanted to simplify my life and free up space for something different and new to happen. I barely slept for four days and nights as I sorted through everything that belonged to me. Even though I had never been a major hoarder it was amazing how much stuff I had accumulated over the years. With each trip to the charity shop it felt as though both physical and emotional space were opening up. I could even think and concentrate more clearly.

Over time as I helped friends and family clear clutter from their homes, I realised I would love to work in this area professionally. In May 2002 I set up No More Clutter to help people declutter and organise their homes. My degree in psychology gives me insight into the reasons people hoard and the obstacles they need to overcome to create the clutter-free home they desire. My work background is organizing information projects for charities. So I enjoy setting up effective systems for anything from laundry to paperwork.

Being a professional declutterer and organiser is still a rarity in the UK, although it is a well-established service in the USA. I find it incredibly rewarding to see an overwhelmed client who feels superglued to their possessions letting go and regaining control of their life and home.

My first major decluttering blitz opened up a whole new chapter in my life. Running No More Clutter has given me many exciting new opportunities – writing for magazines, appearing on radio and TV, and meeting clients from many different walks of life.

My philosophy is simple – I believe your home is a place to be enjoyed every day. Clinging on to endless stuff from your past or oversaving things for the future can stop you making the most of today. I don't believe possessions should weigh us down and cause us misery. They are with us to be used and enjoyed and to enhance our lives.

HOW TO USE THIS BOOK

This book aims to take you from feeling overwhelmed and unsure about how to deal with your clutter to feeling motivated and confident that you can create a clutter-free home. It breaks down the four stages of clearing clutter into manageable steps. It's up to you whether you read the book cover to cover before you start decluttering. If you are feeling inspired, why not try out the mini-challenges and tasks as you go through the book?

The challenges of decluttering are illustrated throughout by using anecdotes from my clients and others who have shared their clutter stories with me. All the stories are true but personal details have been changed to protect confidentiality.

The four stages of clearing clutter

It is important to carry out the four stages in the following order. A common mistake is to start with stage three and rush out to buy storage boxes of all shapes and sizes. But it is only after you have decluttered that you know what you are keeping and what storage is required. Otherwise the storage solutions end up being part of the clutter!

Stage one: Decluttering
The social and psychological background
• The Introduction explores the social and cultural factors prevalent in Britain today which have led us to being a cluttered nation.

- Chapter One looks at the psychological factors that influence hoarding and how they are holding you back.

How to declutter

- Chapter Two looks at the essence of decluttering – the decision-making process.
- Chapter Three gives you a step-by-step procedure for organizing a decluttering session, looking at the best place to start and how long it will take.

Where to start

- Chapter Four takes you on a room-by-room tour of the home.
- Chapter Five looks at the toughest clutter challenges, like sorting out sentimental items.
- Chapter Six tackles people's biggest hurdle – dealing with paper clutter.
- Chapter Seven explores specific life events that trigger decluttering such as moving home or going through a divorce.

Stage two: Getting the unwanted stuff out of your home

Chapter Eight looks at strategies for actually getting the stuff out of your home. Frank's hall had been filled with black binliners for three years waiting for him to organise a car-boot sale. Despite his good intentions he had got stuck at this crucial stage. Whether you decide to sell or donate your unwanted stuff, you need to complete this process as quickly as possible.

Stage three: Storage solutions

My American clients bemoan the fact that British homes have inadequate closets and poorly designed storage. They are right in believing that good storage is an essential part of staying organised and uncluttered. You will need to find places for all the stuff you want to keep. The shops are full of attractive storage solutions, so enjoy yourself. Chapter Nine explores this in more detail.

Stage four: A lifetime of staying clutter-free

Clutter is always with us and needs ongoing management. Chapter Ten looks at new habits and routines you need to acquire to stay clutter-free. Putting them into action will ensure you win the battle against clutter in the long term.

You'll find a Further Information section at the back of the book, which contains addresses of suppliers of useful storage products like vacuum packs and contact details for organizations which can provide help and support.

TAKE THE CLUTTER QUIZ

Here's a quick test to see how cluttered you are. Time how long it takes you to lay your hands on these five common household items . . .

- your passport
- the spare front-door key
- your doctor's phone number
- your last bank statement
- an envelope and stamp

Less than five minutes to find the lot? Fantastic, you're pretty decluttered and efficiently organised. Ask yourself how stressful it felt. Do you think you could improve on your time? Decluttering experts vary on whether they think we should find things in 30 seconds or a minute.

More than five minutes? Chances are you are already wasting time on a daily basis looking for things you've lost. Apply the tips in this book and try the test again in a few weeks – see how your time has improved.

HOW HAS YOUR HOME GOT SO CLUTTERED?

Clutter tends to build up slowly over a long period, until one day it reaches a point where you feel as though your life is descending into chaos. Suddenly everything is breaking down – the toaster has blown, the printer is jammed, you can't find anything. Things are slipping out of control.

Clutter may have invaded every corner of your home, crept behind your sofa, under your bed, and like a virus has spread and spread. Or there may just be one problem area such as your paperwork or your wardrobe. Some people have fastidiously well-organised record collections in alphabetical order yet their bedroom is a no-go area piled high with dirty laundry.

You may look at friends and feel mystified and envious because they have an immaculate home, even with three young kids. Sometimes, though, all is not what it seems. I often go into homes that are obviously well cared for with little visible clutter. Then we start opening cupboards crammed to the hilt with junk and stuff. Lofts and garages are overflowing. Somewhere nearby there is a rented storage unit full of mystery items.

The Clutter Tour

On client visits my starting point is always the Clutter Tour. It shows on a room-by-room basis where the clutter is, how far-reaching it is, what is working well and what is causing frustration and irritation. The Clutter Tour gives me an overall picture of the home and what the client hopes to achieve.

Your task now is to carry out your own Clutter Tour. At this stage you are simply trying to get an overview of the clutter situation in your home and to set goals before you start out on your decluttering journey. Later on, Chapter Four will give you a detailed room-by-room tour with ideas on how to assess each room and turnaround tips for creating clutter-free space.

Arm yourself with a notebook and a camera and step outside your home. As you enter, are you uplifted, or do you feel your spirits sink? Is it easy to move around or is the floor piled high? Wander from room to room and make notes, take photos of any clutter hotspots or inspirational places where everything works. Really look at everything including the furniture and the pictures on your walls. Open drawers and look inside cupboards to complete your assessment of how clutter is affecting your home.

Review what you learnt from the Clutter Tour

Ask yourself: 'If I had a magic decluttering wand, what would I like to achieve?' Do you want a minimal look with clean lines, a country cottage feel or an opulent ambience with rich textiles? Practically, what would make your home life flow more smoothly? Do you want to open the kitchen cupboards without stuff falling out? Do you want to find storage for all your paperwork? Or do you want to claw back space for a loft extension for your growing family? Write down a list of all your decluttering goals.

Come up with a Decluttering Touchstone

To summarise the feeling I want to create in my home I would use the words *space*, *minimal* and *light*. What would your words be? Write them down in your notebook and refer to them often. Keep that vision and your goals in mind and it will guide you throughout the decluttering process.

Where has it all come from?

You may feel helpless faced with the daily onslaught of junk mail, newspapers and miscellaneous stuff that arrives in your home. But most of the things there have been brought in by you or someone you live with. Spend ten minutes going round a room and ask yourself how everything got there.

Stuff you have bought

What percentage of your recent purchases were planned and how many were impulse buys? You may have developed a siege mentality and got into the habit of overbuying food and household goods. You may be a comfort shopper and regularly buy yourself treats to compensate for having a stressful day. Or you may be addicted to the adrenaline buzz of shopping and be surrounded by new purchases, many still in their original wrappings.

You may have a great eye for a bargain and regularly cruise charity shops, car-boot sales and jumble sales. You may find it impossible to resist three-for-two or buy-one-get-one half-price offers. You may be won over by advertising promises for the latest gadget and feel you have to buy it, even though you've already got a houseful. You may be an avid collector and every shelf and surface in your home is crammed full with your treasures.

Free stuff

You may never walk past a skip without rescuing something. Or you may go to conferences where you get free key-rings, pens and other stuff. Who in this world doesn't love a freebie? My heart lifts when I see a free gift – especially bags given away with glossy women's magazines. For me this goes back to childhood when free gifts with comics were a real highlight. I know it's going to end up in the charity bag in a couple of days but the initial rush is still there.

Stuff you have been given

You may be a sentimental hoarder and keep all your birthday and Christmas cards. By the time you reach 40 you'll have boxes and boxes. Probably many of them from people you can't even remember. You may believe it is respectful to keep every gift you're given – whether you like it or not.

Stuff that arrives through your letterbox daily

Paper flows in through the letterbox throughout the day. Most of it is complete junk. However, if it is not immediately binned or recycled, before you know it there's a paper mountain of circulars, take-away menus, cards from cab firms and free newspapers.

Inherited things

You may have inherited possessions from loved ones which many years later are still packed away in their original cardboard boxes. The thought of sorting through them may be deeply upsetting so you keep putting it off. Chapter Five looks at the special challenge of inherited things and Chapter Seven has a section on coping with your loved one's belongings following bereavement.

Stuff other people you live with have brought in

Living with others can cause conflict over who is making the home cluttered. How much of the stuff is your partner's and how much is yours? People comment that kids today have too many things. But this is only a reflection of the sheer volume of possessions most adults have.

Stuff you are storing for another person

Are you providing temporary storage for a friend or family member? If so, have the agreed few weeks turned into months and even years?

Clutter and contemporary living

Now you have a clearer picture of how your home got cluttered, it is important to place this in a wider social context. Why are we facing an epidemic of cluttered homes in Britain today? There are many factors contributing to this phenomenon – let's explore the most significant ones.

Frugality and affluence

Wartime beliefs are still prevalent in the British culture – be frugal, avoid waste and keep things that may come in useful. But overlayering this, we live in affluent, consumer-driven times where new products are constantly zooming on to the market. Both adults and kids are inundated with slick advertising. A mobile phone over a year old is considered a joke. One of the central reasons why British homes are cluttered is because we buy new yet hold on to the old. Your new flat-screen TV has pride of place in the living room yet you feel compelled to shove the old one into the spare room.

Economist Andrew Oswald notes that Britain, like most industrialised nations, is approximately twice as rich as it was as recently as 1960 and almost three times richer than after the war. However, having a lot more material wealth only makes us marginally more happy. Psychologist Oliver James states that we are increasingly stressed 'by wanting what we have not got . . . We obsessively and enviously compare our lot with that of others or against an impossible ideal and find it lacking. It leaves us feeling that there is never enough, depleted and unable to get our lives under control.'

US writer and documentary maker John de Graaf calls this epidemic of overconsumption 'Affluenza – the never-ending search for more'. Anyone with a cluttered home knows that too many things, rather than increasing your happiness, can actually make you feel overwhelmed and miserable.

Busy, stressful lives

Britain is known as the 'long hours' capital of Europe and a survey in 2001 found that more than a third of British employees felt overworked.

A survey by the Chartered Institute of Personnel and Development (October 2003) found that on average a woman's working week is half a day longer than it was five years ago. At the same time 67 per cent of young women between the ages of 18 and 35 said they were unhappy at work. This rises to 83 per cent of 30–35-year-olds.

This 'cash-rich-time-poor' culture has led to the rise in services such as lifestyle management companies. People no longer have the time to organise their own social or domestic lives. Shopping is a release from the stresses of the working day.

There is no longer a strong connection between what we need and what we buy. It is easy to be seduced by clever marketing into buying excess and sometimes useless stuff. The phrase 'Spend it like Beckham' has entered the culture. A recent survey (November 2003) found that average consumer debt in Britain stands at over £6,800 per household, excluding mortgages, which is the highest in Europe. Not only are we buying things we don't need, we are buying luxury goods and designer labels that we cannot afford.

There is a strong correlation between shopping behaviour and clutter. For example, Britons are spending £12.8 billion a year on health and beauty products. Most of my clients have huge stockpiles of half-used and unopened cosmetic or grooming products and stashes of vitamin bottles.

Maureen, with whom I worked recently, said she enjoys the attention from the beauty demonstrators and having the item wrapped in tissue paper and a pretty bag. Sometimes she pretends it's a present so she can have the extra bliss of having it gift-wrapped. She says, 'It's like saying I deserve this, I work hard – so I need some luxury in my life. Although I feel guilty too, because I know I have loads of unopened products at home.'

THE FIVE KEY BENEFITS
OF HAVING A CLUTTER-FREE HOME

Whatever your current lifestyle and circumstances, clearing the clutter from your home will help you cope with the stresses of daily life. Remember that everything you own demands something of you. It demands space in your home, it demands to be looked after – things need cleaning, insuring and maintaining. While you may think out of sight is out of mind, things you hold on to take up mental space. At some unconscious level you know all that junk behind the sofa is waiting to be dealt with.

You will gain a feeling of control and confidence

You will no longer feel as though your stuff owns you. You own it and choose what you keep in your home. Your confidence will increase as you succeed at tackling something you put off and found difficult in the past. Your home will feel cared for and easy to move around. We're not talking about perfect housekeeping, just somewhere you enjoy living.

'It helped me reclaim and begin to reshape my home after my divorce. I no longer needed to treat myself to new makeup and clothes to make myself feel better.' Karen

You will save time

In your busy life, the last thing you want to do is waste time looking for lost stuff. It's been estimated that the average person wastes 150 hours a year looking for lost papers. If everything is organised and in its place, you'll find things effortlessly. The less stuff you have cluttering up the place, the easier it will be to keep it tidy and clean. Fewer knick-knacks mean less dusting!

'Now I've sorted out my filing system and desk I no longer waste time looking for papers while I've got an important client on the phone.' Nick

You'll feel more relaxed and clear-headed

You will feel more relaxed after you organise your home. Clutter can be a block to moving on with your life. When you let go of unwanted stuff from your past it frees you emotionally to face the future with renewed energy. You'll find as you create more space that you are able to think more clearly.

'I feel like some huge block is out of the way and I can finally explore my plans to leave London.' Lucy

You will save money

Knowing what you own and being able to find it quickly will stop you buying duplicates to replace things that are temporarily lost. I've known people buy blenders, cameras and multiple copies of a CD because they can't lay their hand on the original. It will also help you to focus on buying what you need rather than impulse-buying.

'I started to feel less guilty about being a supermum. I stopped compensating my kids with things because I work full-time.' Jane

You will feel energised

Decluttering and creating order out of chaos is enormously liberating. I hear words like 'lighter', 'euphoric' or 'a weight has lifted' over and over again. Relish the space you have created as you enjoy living in the moment more. As you become less attached to material things, you will open yourself up to new experiences flowing through your life.

'I feel like my home can breathe again. I've sent three carloads to charity and I'm not done yet.' Mary

chapter one

The Psychology of Hoarding

The Oxford English Dictionary's definition of 'to hoard' is:
'To collect and hide or store for preservation,
security or future use.'

In this chapter we are going to explore the psychological reasons for hoarding by looking at the following questions. Why do we become hoarders and why does hoarding become a problem? Are there different types of hoarder? What behaviours do hoarders exhibit that stand in the way of a clutter-free home? What triggers a hoarder to wake up one day, decide to buy this book and banish clutter from their home?

WHY DO WE HOARD?

I'm fascinated by hoarding. For some people belongings are a source of comfort and pleasure. For others they have become a cause of irritation and disorder.

Daisy, a true hoarder, collects anything to do with the Christmas holidays. By September her spare room is crammed full of decorations, new rolls of wrapping paper and more Christmas cards than she will use in a lifetime. Despite this she goes on buying and stashing away more and more every year. Daisy is increasingly frustrated that Christmas clutter is taking over her home all year round. She does not understand why she is compelled to carry on collecting. Nor does she know how to stop.

Knowing her history, I believe her hoarding represents her desire to re-create warm feelings of connection to family and friends to compensate for the austerity of Christmases past.

Understanding what is behind your cluttering behaviour will give you insight into counterproductive beliefs that are standing in your way. This will speed up the process of changing and letting go.

Are hoarders made or born?

Randy Frost, Professor of Psychology at the University of Massachusetts, is an expert on hoarding behaviour. He has found that hoarding runs in families. To date, not enough research has been done to ascertain whether there is a genetic component or it is simply a learnt behaviour. Does your family hoard every last nail, button, piece of string, scrap of used wrapping paper and moth-eaten pair of trousers in case they might come in useful one day? If so, while you were growing up you will have learnt it is important to hold on to things.

You will cling to objects that are useless, have had their day or no longer reflect your lifestyle. A common example is keeping pillows indefinitely. In the past feather pillows were high-value items that lasted a lifetime. Now we live in centrally heated homes our pillows are a veritable hotel for dust mites. It had never occurred to Dave to replace his grandmother's yellowed and stained feather pillows. He was amazed to find that his asthma and skin rashes greatly improved when he bought new ones.

We also soak up domestic rituals unquestioningly. This leads to problems when times and behaviours change. Lydia was getting in a terrible muddle with her laundry. The heart of the problem was that she did the washing once a week on a Monday just like her mother had always done. She'd never questioned this even though she only wore clothes and used towels once. Laundry for her mother's generation in the era of twin tubs had been time-consuming and prohibited the use of clean towels daily.

The result for Lydia was a spare room full of dirty clothes. Because her clutter was also leading to chronic disorganization, she could never find anything clean to wear. It seemed quicker and easier for her to buy some new underwear rather than deal with the overwhelming situation at home. When Lydia started to do her laundry three or four times a week her stress levels fell away.

How do our possessions acquire meaning?

All of us invest meaning in and attribute value to our things. Our identity is closely linked with our possessions. As Rachel said, 'I can't possibly let go of my books – they are the map of my life.' Not only do we gain our sense of identity from what we own, other people also assess us by what we wear, how our home looks and what sort of coffee machine we use.

So how does an inanimate object come to acquire so much emotional significance and meaning in your life? From the moment you select the DVD in the shop and hand over the money it belongs to you. It is yours. You have spent good money on this DVD, you have spent time buying it. It has become part of your life. It is for ever connected to this afternoon, this year, the place and the people you watched it with. The longer you keep it the stronger the tie will be – owning it will become part of your identity.

The psychologist Donald Winnicot found that babies need a transitional object such as a teddy or a blanket to act as a comforter at bedtime. This object comes to represent the love and attachment provided by the parent, when they are absent from the baby's room. No matter how tatty or dirty, only this particular object will provide comfort to the baby. This suggests that it is normal to become attached to and gain feelings of security from prized and loved possessions.

How can this attachment to objects get out of hand?

The groundbreaking psychologist Abraham Maslow argued that there is a hierarchy of needs all human beings have to achieve. First, we need to meet our basic needs for food, water and oxygen. After that we need to be safe and free from chaos and fear. Then there is the need for love and belonging. Finally, there is a need for self-esteem and self-actualization which is about following your bliss, doing what you love and living in the way that feels true to you.

Problems start when people get stuck and try to meet higher-order needs for security, love and self-esteem through hoarding belongings rather than forming close relationships or following their dreams. After all, things cannot criticise you or reject you, and generally stay the same in this ever-changing world. Amassing objects can bestow on collectors the sense of worth that was missing from their early life. When things get out of hand the acquiring and maintaining of possessions use up all our energy. Our possessions rule our lives.

But take heart. If your possessions form a strong part of your identity, freeing yourself from them frees you to redefine yourself and move on. This is what decluttering is all about.

Is there a difference
between men and women who hoard?

In homes throughout the land there will be heated arguments about whether men or women are the bigger hoarders. My experience is that when it comes to volume of clutter there is very little difference. However, when it comes to what is being hoarded there are significant differences between the sexes.

Research has found that women and older adults tend to value things such as photos as symbols of personal and family relationships. Men and teenagers tend to be more utilitarian and value objects for what they do. They love their hi-fi and computer equipment, their gizmos and their tools.

Men often think of themselves as collectors rather than hoarders. I was talking to a male journalist the other day and he told me with immense pride what a phenomenal hoarder he was. To him clutter and collections made his home feel lived in. Even today women are under much more social pressure to feel responsible for the upkeep of the home. Wrong as this is, it often means that women feel much more ashamed of the cluttered state of their homes.

The social scientist Michael Gurian has found that men attach less personal identity to the interior of a home. According to his research the male brain takes in less sensory detail, so men do not notice disorder and dust in the way women do.

Certainly the badly housetrained male is a common stereotype in our society, leaving a trail of dirty washing, mugs and computer magazines in his wake. While this is undoubtedly true in a number of cases it is far from the whole truth. I often get calls from men who are in despair at the amount of clutter their wives are harbouring in their family homes. Overall, I believe discomfort with clutter and a craving for domestic order are felt by both men and women today in our society.

LOSING IT ALL

Pause for a moment and think of words that describe the things we own. I am sure there are many more words and expressions you can think of.

material possessions, earthly belongings, worldly goods, assets, stash, stuff, valuables, chattels, effects, property, treasure, resources, baggage, paraphernalia, gear, trappings.

People vary in how materialistic they are and how attached they are to their possessions. What would it feel like suddenly to lose or be divested of everything we own? Answering this question helps clarify the role of things in our lives, how they link to our sense of self and their relative importance to issues like our health, our relationships and well-being.

In 2001 the artist Michael Landy destroyed everything he owned in the world. All he had left at the end was his cat and his girlfriend. In the vacant C&A building in Oxford Street over 7,000 of his carefully catalogued personal possessions, including photos, unique and valuable works of art, family heirlooms, even his socks, were put on an industrial conveyor belt, then dismantled on a production line manned by ten operatives. He called the work *Break Down*. He said, 'I see this as the ultimate consumer choice. Once *Break Down* has finished, a more personal breakdown will commence – life without my self-defining belongings.'

Over 45,000 people watched the systematic destruction over a two-week period. I remember being shocked and at the same time thinking what courage this would take. Even as a minimalist I have possessions I treasure and would feel a deep wrench if I was parted from them. Landy said, 'When I was finished I did feel an incredible sense of freedom, the possibility that I could do anything.'

In 2000 John Freyer was moving to New York City. He wanted to travel light with only what would fit into the boot of his car so he decided to sell his possessions on the internet. He set up a site called *allmylifeforsale.com* linked to the online auction eBay. He held an inventory party where his friends helped him to tag over 600 things. What was so unusual was that he was selling highly intimate possessions like his answer-machine tape, his photos, old address books and even half-used bags of sugar. His honest sales pitches meant bidders felt they were acquiring a fragment of his lifestyle. At the same time he was also challenging the beliefs of a throwaway consumer society.

For Michael Landy and John Freyer this was a choice, a work of art and a personal exploration of the link between who we are and what we own. For others, losing their possessions in a traumatic event like a fire or a burglary can be devastating. People often ask me what I would save from a fire and I always say my blind Cairn terrier, Barney. If my life depended on it, at the end of the day the rest are only things. But if I had time I'd save my CDs and my records. They are my most valued possessions!

People who survive life-threatening illnesses often report changing their attitude to material things. Pat said, 'After I recovered I changed my priorities, cut my hours. All that stuff I'd craved like designer clothes just didn't seem as important any more.'

Asking yourself what you would save in an emergency will illuminate what really matters to you.

EXTREME HOARDING

For a small minority, excess hoarding is a symptom of an illness such as Obsessive Compulsive Disorder or Attention Deficit Disorder. I was fascinated by the BBC's programme *The Life of Grime* about Mr Trebus who threw absolutely nothing away. He ended up living in a tiny corner of one room with every inch of his garden and large home crammed full of junk. Frequently people with extreme hoarding habits do not see it as a problem – it's more common for their loved ones or neighbours to seek help.

Extreme hoarding is defined by the Los Angeles Mental Health Department as 'the excess collection and retention of things until they interfere with day-to-day functions such as home, health, family, work and social life. Severe hoarding causes health and safety hazards.'

If you or anyone you know matches this definition, consult the Further Information section for sources of professional help.

THE EIGHT TYPES OF HOARDER

While everyone has their unique history, I find hoarders generally fall into a small number of groups. In the course of my work I have noted eight different types of hoarder. You will probably find that you have characteristics of more than one type but predominantly fit into one category. Knowing why you are holding on to certain things will help you challenge old beliefs and give you a reference point for times when you are finding it hard to let go. Hopefully it will also give you insight into what is driving your partner or flatmate's behaviour.

Rainy-day Hoarder

After hard times like the Second World War, redundancy or downsizing after a divorce you may be haunted by the fear of lean periods recurring. We live in an age with few certainties and little job security, high divorce rates and threats of terrorism. One response is to squirrel things away for a rainy day.

Rainy-day beliefs can lead to hoarding useless items such as margarine cartons, old newspapers or used envelopes. This hoarding behaviour is dominated by the idea that 'It might come in useful one day.' A defective electric fire is shoved into the garage along with a broken lawn-mower, old dried-out paint tins and a lot of other junk. If you hoard worthless items, ask yourself whether these things really add to your sense of security. Take the electric fire and lawn-mower to the council tip where at least the metal can be recycled and re-used instead of cluttering up your home.

If a siege mentality develops, your cupboards will be crammed full with supplies for every eventuality. You will keep on buying regardless of how much you already have at home. Try to relax a little – at the end of the day, if hard times come around it will make very little difference whether you have two or ten bottles of washing-up liquid.

Sentimental Hoarder

Joan contacted me recently because her home was overrun with birthday and Christmas cards going back 40 years. Not only did she keep her own cards, she also kept her husband's and every card sent to her five children. She wanted to get a grip on this hoarding yet was heartbroken at the thought of parting with even one card.

Do you hoard all your children's artwork, every photo you've ever taken, every postcard you've ever received, faded mementoes from holidays, your childhood school books, old theatre programmes and artefacts from every job you've ever done? If so, you are a sentimental hoarder.

Memories are an incredibly important part of our lives. Holding on to tangible reminders fends off the fear of losing significant memories. The key to moving on is to be sentimental but selective. Let's face it, Joan doesn't need to keep her husband's cards. It's up to him to decide whether he wants to keep any of them.

Letting go of the least significant memorabilia from your past allows space in your life for new experiences and memories to come along.

Frugal Hoarder

We all like getting our money's worth out of a purchase. Each individual will define good value in a different way. If you are a movie star you can afford to wear an evening dress once. However, if you are frugal you will use a towel for many years until it is scratchy, faded and holey, then cut it up and use it as a rag. The downside is you are denying yourself the pleasure of a fluffy, luxurious towel. The old one could have been recycled or turned into rags years earlier and still not gone to waste.

Once you've spent money it's spent. No amount of guilt will change this fact. Last year as you wandered down the high street those silver sandals called out to you. OK, you only wore them once, they hurt your feet and don't go with anything in your wardrobe. But you keep them because they cost you over £100. Try cutting your losses and donating them to charity. Or recoup some of the money by selling them through a dress agency. Keeping them at the back of the wardrobe unworn for the next five years is not the best option! Don't pay the other price of clutter – taking up valuable storage space in your home for things you will never use again.

There is a vogue for TV programmes showing how to turn your antiques and collectables into cash. Frugal hoarders have an eye on the future and believe many household items will one day be starring on eBay or *Antiques Roadshow*. Low-value items such as cereal packets featuring the Simpsons are stashed away in case they ever become valuable. Ask yourself whether this really makes you feel financially secure. I am not denying that if you hold on to enough stuff some of it will be worth something eventually. But in the meantime, do you really want to turn your home into a cluttered storeroom? Is it fair to ask your partner to live this way? Living clutter-free is all about enjoying your life and home today.

Anxious Hoarder

According to Randy Frost, people who hoard are deeply perfectionist. Do you set yourself very high standards? Do you find it extremely difficult to declutter anything in case you make a mistake and end up regretting your choice? Do you feel too anxious to throw away a ten-year-old gas bill for a house you no longer live in? Do you feel compelled to keep complete records of your life, whether it is bank statements going back to the 1970s or every letter you've ever received?

Your challenge is to learn to trust your choices. If you are an anxious hoarder, start by letting go of one thing every day for a week. That way you will see that nothing terrible happens. As your confidence builds, increase the number of objects you declutter each day. Many of my clients find that once they get into the swing of shredding and recycling ancient paperwork, the whole experience is truly liberating.

Lowering your standards will really help too. Let go of the fantasy of a perfect, spotless home with everything in place 100 per cent of the time. I doubt anyone meets these standards unless they have a team of staff working for them round the clock.

Nesting Hoarder

Do you find that surrounding yourself with things gives you a deep sense of emotional security? Do modern minimal homes leave you cold? Do you like to look around your home and see all your treasured possessions on display?

After a period of material deprivation or a time of emotional trauma such as bereavement it's normal to want to be surrounded by abundance and memories. If you have been hurt or bruised by life, beloved possessions feel safe – you can trust them not to harm you.

If you work in an office, look at how people create a nest around their desks by forming a semi-circle with objects on the floor and on window-sills, with papers stacked high – surrounding and enveloping the space. I often see people do this with their bed or sofa so it feels cosy and enclosed.

This becomes a problem when possessions are so numerous and oppressive that it feels as though they are sucking the very oxygen from your home. Your aim is to start to create some clear space. Nesting hoarders often feel panicky if space is opened up too quickly, so clear a window-sill or a table and see how it feels. Next day, try putting back fewer objects than before. Who knows, you might even enjoy the clear space and leave it like that!

Trophy Hoarder

I was listening to a group of young lads in the pub talking about their computer keyboards and listing all their special features. They were desperate to impress each other with who had the most up-to-the-minute one.

It is part of being human to care what other people think of you. We judge other people by what they wear, what they own and by their lifestyle. Sociologist Juliet Schor's studies have shown that women buy expensive makeup because they don't want to be seen using a £1.99 lipstick from the supermarket.

Your home is one of the most visible ways of showing your status, your lifestyle choices and your taste. When visitors come to your home you want them to be impressed. Victorian houses were always built with the parlour at the front to show off the family's wealth and most expensive possessions.

Do you keep things such as coffee-table books on display because you want to give a glossy impression? Do you keep unopened classics on your bookshelves so others will see you are well-read? Do you hold on to carrier bags from Harrods or DKNY? Do you have to buy the latest flat-screen TV, designer clothing or gizmo to keep up with your friends and family?

If you are holding on to things simply to impress others, it's time to be honest with yourself. If debt is looming large on your horizon, think hard before acquiring one more lifestyle purchase. Instead, create the home you love and your passion and flair will shine through for all to see.

Magpie Hoarder

Magpies love to collect objects. Magpies love abundance, creativity and adding new gems to their hoard. If a friend is chucking out a side-table they volunteer to give it a new home. They adore car-boot sales, rooting out treasure from skips, the cut and thrust of the January sales. They love the buzz of acquiring stuff, the thrill of hunting down a bargain. They show off their new prizes with pride.

Instead of thinking of themselves as hoarders they like to see themselves as collectors. They collect clothing for fancy dress, an array of craft materials or old computers to customise later. Often they have multiple collections on the go at once. Even when their enthusiasm for collecting old beer bottles wanes, the bottles remain gathering dust on the kitchen shelves. Now they're fired up collecting early computer games.

Do you find it hard to resist adding new treasures to your home even if it is stuffed to the rafters? Then you are a magpie. You can still have a lot of fun with your things – but you don't want to end up swamped by your possessions. Slow down your knee-jerk response and evaluate more clearly before bringing home every alluring object you come across. No home will ever be big enough to contain it all.

Rebellious Hoarder

Are you still rebelling against childhood restrictions and deprivations? As a child, did you hate being told to tidy your room? As a young girl, Mary vowed that when she grew up she'd live the way she wanted, in whatever mess she created. It's just that now it's hard to move around her home and, aged 40, she is really sick of living in constant disorder.

Or did you feel your parents deprived you of a Walkman, a TV in your room, a five-speed bike or pink sparkly shoes? Now you have your own money, are you making up for lost time and trying to right old hurts? Has it led to a flat stuffed with gizmos or a leaning tower of shoe boxes that looms over your bedroom?

Your rebellion may be going on at an unconscious level, so if this rings a bell with you spend a few minutes thinking back to your childhood. See if you are deliberately opposing your family's values on tidiness and material possessions. Gaining insight will help you to start thinking about how you want to live today.

TEN TYPICAL HOARDING HABITS

Now you've understood more about what kind of hoarder you are, let's look at counterproductive habits and beliefs that stand in the way of a clutter-free home.

1. Procrastinating

The road to a cluttered home is paved with good intentions, abandoned New Year's resolutions and all those Sunday mornings when you wandered into your junk-filled spare room and fled to have another cup of coffee. The only way to clear clutter is to start today and to keep the momentum going.

Maria Bustillos, who runs a specialist online auction for collectors, makes the point that hoarders 'are not so much anxious to keep stuff as they are to avoid dealing with it'.

Procrastination can take many forms:

- Every time you dump a carrier bag by the front door 'just for now'.
- Every time you put off opening your post or paying your bills 'until tomorrow'.
- Every time you fling something into the spare room rather than deciding whether you still need it.
- Every time you put decluttering into the 'too hard basket' and walk away.

Habit-breaker Spend a couple of minutes doing one thing you have been putting off. Whether it's opening the post, paying a bill or taking your workbag up to your home office, do it now.

2. Having an all-or-nothing attitude

Do you hold inflexible beliefs such as that once you own a book you will keep it for ever, no matter what? Even if the pages yellow and fall out, it is complete trash or a travel book from the 1980s? Even if books are piled in every corner of your home gathering dust and your garage is filled with boxes of books that haven't seen the light of day since you moved six years ago? Even then, do you bristle if anyone suggests your collection seems to be dominating your life and home?

This is familiar territory for me. Clients often start sessions by warning me that they will not part with a single book. As I get to know them I challenge this. I've yet to work with anyone who uses all their cookbooks. Once they realise I'm not out to throw away their beloved collection of *TinTin* annuals or contemporary fiction, they relax and feel able to donate their detective novels and the book on pressure-cooking they've never used.

Habit-breaker Find one collection that is beginning to take over your home. It could be shoes, books, CDs, videos or DVDs. If you choose shoes, search out one pair that you will never wear again. Put them into the charity bag. Sleep on your choice overnight. Unless you wake up at 3 a.m. sweating and thinking you have to keep them, leave them where they are and see if next day you can't declutter a few more!

3. Treating all possessions as equally valuable

If you are a real hoarder you will attach value and meaning to unimportant things such as circulars, old newspapers, snagged tights and business cards from people you can't even remember. Meanwhile, all your true treasures such as your photos, your brand-new jumper, your baby's first shoes are getting lost and crumpled under a heap of junk.

Habit-breaker Start separating the clutter from the treasure. It won't hurt as much as you think. Find and chuck out the following five things:

• one rusty piece of cutlery
• one pair of tired socks
• one T-shirt that will never be white again
• one out-of-date magazine
• one take-away menu you'll never use

Have a good look before you get rid of it. This is true clutter. Trust me, you will not miss any of it.

4. Being easily distracted

You set aside the morning to organise your clothes while your son is at nursery. As you drag out all the junk lurking at the bottom of your wardrobe, you find the charger for the mobile phone you lost last week. So you wander off to the kitchen to put the phone on charge. While you are there you riffle through your junk drawer and come across a half-read letter from your friend in York. You'd forgotten about it, so you make a quick cup of tea and settle down to read it. Fantastic news! She's coming to London in three weeks so you decide to send her a quick email. Might as well check your inbox at the same time. There's a great offer on DVDs. So you have a quick browse and order a couple.

By the end of the morning the mess from the wardrobe is still out on the bedroom floor, all the junk from the kitchen drawer is out on the counter, it's time to pick up your son and things are worse than before!

Habit-breaker Set a kitchen timer for ten minutes and make sure you are still in the same room doing the same task that you set out to do.

5. Sabotaging your efforts

There are often powerful emotional reasons for staying cluttered. If you are unconsciously afraid of change you will repeatedly sabotage your efforts to get organised.

As well as procrastinating, being a perfectionist and easily distracted, there are many other ways to undermine your attempts to declutter your home. Here are some I've come across.

- Do you focus on how much there is still left to do, instead of being pleased with what you have achieved?
- Do you feel overwhelmed with shame, find yourself constantly apologizing to others and calling yourself derogatory names, such as lazy or slovenly?
- Do you throw away essential things to subvert progress? Hannah gave away her only winter coat in January. Shivering in her denim jacket confirmed her worst fears – you are bound to miss things once they are gone. This gave her full

justification to delay any further decluttering for a few more months 'to avoid another mistake'.

• Do you end up making things worse every time you try to declutter? As well as learning and practising the skills in this book, make sure you are not angry with anyone in your life who is putting pressure on you to change.

Habit-breaker Today I want you to complete one small decluttering task. Choose between sorting out your workbag, cutlery drawer, bedside table or one shelf of books. Keep going until it is finished. Now stand back and admire your work. Congratulate yourself on learning a new skill and tackling something you previously found difficult. Your reward is to buy yourself a bunch of flowers. Every time you look at them, remind yourself how you're on your way to the clutter-free home you deserve.

6. Multi-tasking instead of focusing on one thing at a time

When it comes to clearing clutter, multi-tasking does not work. Decluttering requires your full attention on the job. It will work only if you focus on one object and one decision at a time.

If you are incredibly busy it may feel indulgent to carve out uninterrupted time to sort out your stuff. Motivate yourself by remembering how much time you waste losing things and being disorganised. It is better to spend five minutes' exclusive time decluttering than a scattered hour while you are trying to deal with calls, domestic chores or your kids' demands.

Habit-breaker Find a quiet time of day – it may be first thing in the morning or before you go to bed – and practise five minutes' concentrated decluttering. You'll be amazed by what you can achieve.

7. Wanting clutter to sort itself out

Jeff said to me recently, 'Decluttering doesn't work – all those piles of paper that we sorted out have come back.' As we chatted it became clear he hadn't filed or thrown away a single piece of paper for three months. He'd 'forgotten' all the maintenance routines we'd talked about.

As Joan Rivers said, 'I hate housework! You make the beds and you do the dishes – and six months later you have to start all over again.'

Unless you downshift and opt out of modern life and consumerism, it's hard to stop clutter entering your life. Part of getting to grips with it is coming to terms with the notion that you will have to deal with it in the long term.

Habit-breaker Let go of the magic wand fantasy that will banish clutter for ever and freeze your home in a perfect clutter-free state. Start putting the tips in this book into action. That way clutter will no longer be running your life.

8. Putting other people first

The ugly and unloved table in your hallway makes your spirits plummet every time you look at it. Your mum gave it to you when she moved and it used to be a favourite of hers. In your bid not to offend her you've ended up keeping it and putting her feelings before your own.

I know it's a delicate situation. But tell her you are restyling your hallway and offer to give the table back. Don't let feelings of guilt pressure you into keeping something that you detest. It's your home, your taste, your life.

Habit-breaker Find one unwanted gift you can't stand. You may feel deeply uncomfortable and disloyal, so choose something ephemeral like bubble bath or yellow socks. As you put it into the charity bag, take a deep breath and reclaim your right to keep only things you love and use.

9. Acquiring too much stuff

As we saw in the Introduction, things don't miraculously appear in your home. There is a direct correlation between how much stuff you bring in and how cluttered your home becomes. If you are a compulsive shopper this is not going to be easy to change. At this stage all you're trying to do is take control in one small area. If you buy a DVD every Saturday make this the week you rent one instead. Or if you always buy something new to wear at the weekend, fish out something you've never worn from your wardrobe.

When I discuss this with my clients they look deeply pained. They fear they have entered a joyless era of deprivation. But remember, the aim is to break the compulsive part of shopping, not the fun part.

Habit-breaker If you always overbuy magazines, cosmetics or DVDs, this week choose one type of product, whichever is your personal addiction, and don't buy any.

10. Blocking the flow in the home

Clutter can form a physical barrier to moving freely around and accessing storage. Using the floor and every available surface as a dumping ground is cluttering behaviour. This leads to a feeling of struggle and stagnation that often echoes the inner world of the hoarder.

Jane did not want to face up to the stuff in her spare bedroom. So she piled boxes, bags and miscellaneous junk in front of the door. Once we had fought our way in we found the fitted wardrobes were also blocked with more binliners. Jane did not have a clue what was in her wardrobe. As the clutter mountain subsided we uncovered designer suits, bed-linen still in its wrapper and many other treasures lurking among the clutter. The valuable storage space we freed up meant there was room for all the possessions she wanted to keep. After reclaiming her spare room she went ahead with her plan to set up a home office and work there one day a week. Now her space was clear she was free to move on with her life.

Habit-breaker Tackle the floor in your hallway. Remove any bags, coats, piles of newspapers that are clogging up the space. Once you are done, come back in through the front door. How much better does it feel now the space has been opened up?

TRIGGERS FOR DECLUTTERING

'When people go on holiday and are in relatively clutter-free environment it releases their spirit and their mind. Then they come back and have this incubus of clutter reattached to them and they can't think why they aren't

enjoying that freedom of spirit they had when they were on holiday. I think possessions creep up on you and pull you down.' Sir Terence Conran (2003)

So what makes someone wake up one morning and decide today is the day they will free themselves from all that stuff? What makes them want to challenge the hoarding habits of a lifetime? There are many triggers but I would break these down into three categories:

• **Significant life events** such as moving home, having a baby, setting up a home office, a landmark birthday, divorce or moving in with a partner are an ideal time to re-evaluate your life. Letting go of old stuff will free you to move on and really get the best out of this new phase of your life.

'I'm about to turn thirty and I'm fed up of living like a student. I decided it was time to junk the chipped mugs, scruffy clothes and cuddly toys. I'm sick of people being rude about the state of my flat. Decluttering is my birthday present to myself.' Ruth

• **Pressure from others.** Living with someone who hoards can be very stressful, particularly if you like order and tidiness. It is not uncommon for clients to phone when clutter is beginning to cause serious relationship problems.

'My wife can't stand all my collections, she feels like there is no space for her to relax in our house. She keeps threatening if I don't sort it out I'll come home one day and find it all in a skip. Rather than get a divorce I know it's time to sell some stuff on eBay.' Phil

- **Reaching the end of your tether.** You wake up one morning and want your life to be less stressful and more fun. You're fed up wasting time and energy and letting your possessions rule your life.

  'I took two hours to find my car insurance, was late for a meeting and I was so frustrated and drained I knew it was time for a change.' Mark

chapter two

Decluttering Decisions

The essence of decluttering is choosing whether to keep something or let it go. It sounds incredibly simple, doesn't it? So why is it difficult to decide whether to keep an old tartan blanket? As we saw in Chapter One, our possessions are not inanimate objects without meaning. They are linked to our memories, our sense of identity, our beliefs about getting value and use out of things. They feel as though they are part of us. As we look at the blanket, we see our grandmother's home, we remember it being on our bed when we visited every summer. It may be worn and frayed but it evokes happy feelings.

Last week's Sunday paper is still lying unread on the coffee table. We worry we'll waste money and miss out on great articles if we throw it away. We look at piles of recipe cards from magazines and imagine that one day we'll have time to try them out.

Stand back at this point and recall your goals from the Clutter Tour. If you want to create more space, you will have to let some things go. It's not an all-or-nothing process. It's about being honest, simplifying and streamlining your life. It's not about carelessly chucking out precious memories. Keep and cherish the beloved blanket – it is true treasure. On the other hand, unread newspapers quickly become piles of clutter.

WHY ARE YOU KEEPING THIS?

The key question I always ask a client who is staring at a watch they have never worn is, 'Why are you keeping this?' Your task is to focus on each item in turn and ask yourself the same question. If you are dithering about something it helps to clarify things by asking yourself more in-depth questions.

- Have I used it in the last year?
- If I lost it would I buy another one to replace it?
- Did I even remember owning it before I came across it?
- Does it remind me of happy times in my life?
- Does looking at it or using it give me pleasure?
- Does it reflect my life and the home I want to create today?
- Does this item of clothing fit me now and do I feel good in it?

If you answered **NO** to any of these questions, it's time to say goodbye. If you are still not sure, ask yourself, does it pass the Smile Test?

The Smile Test

Your pink shoes pass the Smile Test – you just have to smile because you feel so good in them! A photo of you drinking champagne on your 30th birthday reminds you of a great evening with friends. As Deanna picks up her childhood book about insects, her whole face lights up. The Smile Test tells you when something is real treasure. Even practical things like wine glasses and mugs should be a pleasure to use and pass the Smile Test.

Stay tuned in to your reactions for warning signs that you feel unhappy or negative about an item. People often start sighing when they hold up something they feel ambivalent about. Or they give long, complicated explanations of why they *should* keep something, even though they never use it and do not like it.

Paula was keeping old love letters in her wardrobe from a man who had brought a lot of misery into her life. She could not bear even to handle them, let alone re-read them. So she asked me to shred them. Letting go meant she was literally no longer giving him space in her home or her heart.

You deserve to surround yourself with beloved possessions and warm associations from your past. Junk bad memories like rejection letters from interviews and you will let go of a lot of negativity in your life.

BLOCKS TO DECISION-MAKING

Beware catastrophic fantasies

If you feel panicky at the thought of letting something go, perhaps you are afraid of making a mistake. Ask yourself: what is the worst that could happen? This will help you get a sense of perspective on letting go of an old calendar from 1983. Trust me – the sky will not fall in.

It does take time to adjust to changes in your environment. For a short while after you've given something away it is as though the ghostly presence is still there. During this period you may look for the object out of habit and feel a pang because it is gone. I call this phenomenon 'ghosting'. After a couple of weeks you adjust and it's unlikely you'll ever think about it again.

Considering the hundreds of bags I've given to charity shops over the years I've only ever missed a few CDs. None of us has the space to keep all the possessions we acquire in a lifetime. Balance your apprehensions against the positive improvements to be gained as you restore order in your life.

Watch out for overload

Occasionally someone I'm working with gets so sick of all the stuff they have accumulated that they want to chuck everything out. My job then is to calm them down and prevent them throwing away things they will regret. So if you feel yourself tipping over into the mindset where you want to throw away every single thing you own, walk away for a while and take a breather. Wait until you can distinguish again between clutter and the things you truly value.

Deeper blocks

If you find it hard to make decisions in general or become chronically stressed or anxious about each object, this may be due to underlying medical conditions such as Obsessive Compulsive Disorder (OCD), Attention Deficit Disorder (ADD) or depression. Harriet, who suffers from ADD, remarked how cluttered modern living is a nightmare for her. She said, 'If only I'd lived a rural life in the nineteenth century I would not have had to deal with so many things and endless information. It would have been so much easier to manage.'

Clutter and depression can become part of a vicious cycle where the stress of living a disorganised life can add to feelings of hopelessness or ineffectiveness. If you think there are underlying problems, do seek professional advice rather than struggle on unsuccessfully on your own.

KEY THINGS TO REMEMBER BEFORE YOU START

I want to level with you about the realities of decluttering because I think the more practically and honestly you approach it, the more likely you are to succeed. Keeping these ideas in mind will help you to make decisions about what to keep and what to let go.

Every home can only hold so much

One definition of clutter is owning too much stuff for the space you live in. Even with the most creative use of storage there are limits on how much any home can hold. This is true whether you live in a studio flat or a five-bedroom house, whether you have a single wardrobe or a walk-in one. My clients with larger homes struggle with clutter at least as much as those with small flats.

Playing the numbers game pays dividends

If you live in a city-centre flat with a small kitchen it is unlikely you'll have space for an elaborate dinner service. However, we all need useful things like mugs. Your aim is to choose a number that suits your lifestyle and then stick to it. Work out how many mugs you need by calculating the number of people living in your home and how much entertaining you do. Once you've decided on 14 mugs, keep to that number.

Tastes and lifestyles change

Over the years as your lifestyle changes it's normal for your attachment to particular possessions to alter. The black coffee table that was so cutting-edge ten years ago now looks tired and dated. Your videos are gathering dust since the arrival of your state-of-the-art DVD player. Your youngest kid has started school but you still have a loft full of baby paraphernalia.

Take a step back and look at things with fresh eyes. A decade ago I loved floral tea sets – I even had the odd tea party. Now I prefer plain white china, and if you come to my home you'll get your tea in a mug!

Honesty is vital

If you are a busy working parent, do you really have time to make jam? If not, recycle all those jam jars and don't feel guilty. Your plan to design and handmake your cards never quite happened, so pass on the craft materials to someone who will use them. If you haven't played squash for 20 years, why are you still keeping all the gear? Are you honestly going to play again? That expression 'Use it or lose it' applies here. Set yourself a deadline of a couple of months and if you haven't played by then, give the racquets away.

Decluttering can be an emotional roller-coaster

You will come across possessions which will trigger old memories. Some will be happy and some will remind you of low points in your life. You may experience strong emotions and feel tearful, panicky, guilty, euphoric, relieved or energised. After a bereavement, divorce or trauma, sorting through possessions will be particularly difficult. If you choose to work alone, make sure that there is someone on the end of the phone who can offer support. Whatever your situation, be kind to yourself and don't beat yourself up because you haven't dealt with this stuff in the past. Be pleased and proud of yourself because you are tackling it now.

Minimalism doesn't suit everyone

We all have a different comfort zone for how many possessions we need to feel secure. I've seen clients unnerved by too much open space created in a session. They only calm down when they've found a few objects to 'cosy it up' again.

Millie, who is a serious hoarder, said, 'In the war I had three dresses. One on my back, one in the wash and one in the wardrobe. Now I have more clothes than I can wear in my lifetime.' Because of her history she will always associate minimalism with hard times. Nevertheless, her overcrowded home is making her deeply uncomfortable.

Everything you own takes up both physical and mental space. Ask yourself this fundamental question: is this much stuff making your life better? If the answer is no, aim to create a warm environment with just the right amount of possessions to make you feel relaxed and truly at home.

Decluttering can be really good fun

Clients often say to me, 'I didn't realise decluttering was going to be fun.' As you unearth lost things, think of yourself as on a treasure hunt. Instead of berating yourself for shopping mistakes, have a laugh about it. We all make crazy choices. I recently went out on a boiling hot summer's day and bought a pair of trousers that were only £20 in the sales. It's just a shame they didn't fit very well! Enjoy reliving happy memories as you come across your puffball skirt from the 1980s or your collection of football cards.

Making broader category decisions helps

Decluttering involves lots of decisions so it helps enormously if you make bigger category decisions like letting go of:

- all chick-lit novels
- all theatre programmes
- all clothes that are too big or have been unworn in the last year

- your entire collection of clip-on earrings
- all eggcups if you never eat boiled eggs

Streamlining similar items reduces clutter

When you've gathered up similar things from different corners of your home you'll see how many umbrellas, guide books to Paris, staplers and cameras you own. Ask yourself how many of each item you need and use? Do you have room to store them?

Common sense comes in here. If you have five umbrellas, hold on to them all if, like most of us, you have a tendency to lose them. But what use are four out-of-date guides to Paris? Keep the most recent and lose the rest. Uma had 11 cameras – the confusion caused by all the different attachments, cases, film sizes and instruction manuals was causing her stress. We decided she needed just two – a lightweight one to take on holiday and a more sophisticated one for home use. The rest could be given to charity or sold.

Living with others is a special challenge

Clutter and hoarding can cause enormous stress and bad feeling between partners. It is easy to blame each other for the mess and to resent each other's collections and hoarding habits. The best way to approach decluttering is always to concentrate on sorting your own stuff even if your partner is a hoarder. Never get rid of other people's belongings without their permission. Think how you would feel if someone chucked out things that matter to you. Of course it would make you angry. Under pressure, true hoarders cling even harder to their possessions. Instead, focus on sorting out your own clutter and you may be pleasantly surprised to find that your partner follows your example. Couples issues are discussed more fully in the Moving in Together section of Chapter Seven.

Living with children can present huge challenges for parents as kids and clutter seem to go hand in hand. One of Karen's worst nightmares was that her two-year-old son would follow in his father's footsteps. The thought of living with two hoarders was too much for her. She was determined to get her son accustomed to decluttering as soon as possible. Kids are often attached to strange objects that look like junk. So let them decide what goes and what stays.

Living in a shared house with flatmates can also be a challenging situation. In my 20s I shared a house in North London. One of my male flatmates was obsessively tidy, with a zero-tolerance for disorder and mess. Every time we were relaxing in front of the TV, he would appear with his rubber gloves on, hoovering and tidying up around us. If you share with others, look at how you can create clutter-free communal zones in your home and leave people to do as they like in their own rooms.

Other people may be ambivalent

It's up to you whether you discuss decluttering at the early stages with family and friends. In an ideal world they would wholeheartedly support your desire for a more organised life. Unfortunately this is not always the case. Change can be unsettling and people close to you may express some ambivalence or even hostility.

It is better to work on your own at first as friends and family members are likely to get emotionally involved. They often have strong feelings about what you should and should not keep. Remember, it is your home and your stuff and you do not need anyone's permission to let go of things that belong to you.

Decluttering is a process

Decluttering generally happens in stages. Streamlining your possessions is like taking off old wallpaper – each time you do it you discover more and more layers of stuff you no longer need. Take it at your own pace. You may not be ready to let go of all your miniature bottles or detective novels at once. Put away a couple of your least favourite ones for a week and if you don't miss them, continue to weed them out. As you get used to a more uncluttered way of life it will get more comfortable to let things go, I promise.

chapter three

How to Organise a Decluttering Session

So far we've explored Britain's consumer culture, the nation's hoarding habits and how to make decluttering decisions. It is now time to take action and actually deal with the clutter that is clogging up your home. This chapter outlines the nuts and bolts of how to organise a session. Whether you declutter for five minutes at a time or all day long the same principles apply. Whatever pace you work at, if you follow these procedures you'll make fantastic progress.

People I meet often ask my advice on the best way to go about getting their home organised. The most common questions are: how long does it take, where on earth do I start, and how do I actually do it? Let's look at each of these in turn.

HOW LONG DOES IT TAKE?

There is no TV makeover magic or quick fix to sort clutter. Your home did not become cluttered overnight therefore it's going to take time to declutter it. How long will depend on the quantity of stuff you own (including hidden 'cupboard clutter'), how easy you find it to make decisions and how much time you have available.

It's normal to underestimate how long projects take, so be realistic and overallow for each job. Even if you only tackle one area a week, make decluttering a priority in your life. Commit to persevering until you have achieved the clutter-free home you desire.

WHERE IS THE BEST PLACE TO START?

Someone emailed me recently and asked, 'Is it better to start upstairs or downstairs when I clear clutter?' The answer is, it doesn't matter. What counts is that you build confidence by successfully completing easy projects like your cutlery drawer. Finish each job before moving on to another and never reclutter any area you have cleared.

I often find people hell-bent on tackling the most difficult areas of their home like the loft or a five-year backlog of paperwork. My advice is to start somewhere less daunting. If you start with the heavy-duty stuff, you can lose your way before you see the benefits. Always start small and work up – that way success leads to success.

DIFFERENT DECLUTTERING APPROACHES

Here are the options available to you for organizing a decluttering session:

- Work in **time slots** – choose from five minutes to all day long. Get to know your own physical and emotional limits for decluttering. If you work best in one-hour slots, do that.
- Work on a **room-by-room** basis – even then, break each job down into separate components – take it literally one drawer or shelf at a time. Chapter Four will guide you round the home.
- Work by **sorting similar objects** – so today go through your sunglasses and tomorrow repeat the process with your computer games.

Five-minute mini-challenges

If even the thought of decluttering sends you into a cold sweat, begin with a daily five-minute mini-challenge. These are useful to get you going and have the great benefit of giving immediate reward. Use your kitchen timer to get you underway. Mini-challenges are fun and they do work.

- Gather up all pens and biros. Scribble with them and chuck the defunct ones.
- Collect all the loose change and foreign coins lying around. Charity shops will be glad of them.
- Go into each room and find one object you no longer want to keep.
- Clear out your handbag or briefcase. Weigh it before and after you've lightened your load.
- Go on a hunt and see how many odd socks you can find.
- Clear out the glove compartment of your car.
- Scan your bookshelves for books you'll never read again or out-of-date travel guides.

- Gather up old newspapers for recycling or the bin. Don't start reading them!
- Have a look under your bed and see what you find there.
- Take out-of-date notices off your noticeboard.
- Count how many mugs you own. Then decide how many you actually use and need. Let go of the spare ones and any chipped ones.
- Flick through unopened junk mail and recycle or bin.
- Dare to look in a cupboard or drawer you haven't been in for a while. Remind yourself what's in there.
- Go through your herbs and spices – chuck any past their sell-by date.

Moving up from the mini-challenge to a regular longer slot

Once you feel comfortable with the mini-challenges, set aside anything from ten minutes to an hour at a time and start with the jobs you find easiest. Ideally, do some decluttering every day, but if this is not practical, make a date in your diary every few days. It helps to set goals like having friends over for drinks when you've cleared your living space. Tick off each small project as you complete it to underline how much you are achieving. Incentives like employing a cleaner or getting your bedroom redecorated when the worst of the clutter is out of the way will also keep you motivated.

Good places to start are:

- your linen cupboard
- underwear drawer
- bathroom cabinet

- bedside table
- magazine rack
- cookbooks and gardening books – you know you don't use them all

Moving on to the blitz method

Once you are confident of your decluttering stamina, consider a faster, more intensive method. The decluttering blitz is a great way to transform your home quickly. Set aside a weekend or take a couple of days off work. Once you get into the swing of it you'll find time flies by, so work for as long as you can each day. If you have a deadline looming such as moving home, the Blitz Method may be for you.

I usually work with clients for four hours a day. For some clients this is plenty, but others are so fired up they carry on for several hours on their own. Make it easier by playing your favourite music, and take frequent breaks for a snack and a cup of tea – you'll need it! Remember, too, the more stuff you have, the more you need to pace yourself.

HOW IS DECLUTTERING ACTUALLY DONE?

To get started you'll need a few basic supplies, a period of uninterrupted time and a plan for getting unwanted stuff out of the house. Then it's a question of following the 12-point decluttering plan and powering through to success even when things get difficult.

Gather your supplies together

- basic cleaning materials
- strong black binliners for rubbish
- coloured binliners (I always use blue) for charity. Using coloured binliners makes it easy to distinguish charity bags from the rubbish bags
- small cardboard boxes and newspapers for fragile items
- an old sheet to use as a dust cover
- a laundry basket to rehome things
- a recycling box or bag
- a notebook and pen
- office supplies such as sticky labels (see Chapter Six for details) for organizing your paperwork

Earmark a period of time

Decluttering requires concentration, so you will need an undisturbed stretch of time without distractions. Switch off your phone, your computer and TV. If you live with others, choose a time when your partner or housemate is away and your kids are being looked after by someone else.

Ella, a working mum, told me how difficult she had found it to allocate time for decluttering. Her long working hours combined with looking after two children meant that finding a chunk of free time was a challenge. At the end of a long, hard day all she wanted to do was relax and put her feet up. She solved the problem by trading baby-sitting on a Saturday morning with an equally cluttered single mother. On alternate weekends they got space to themselves to sort things out. The added bonus was that they were able to give each other emotional support and have a laugh about some of the absurd things they had been holding on to.

Remind yourself that even five minutes' decluttering will make a difference. You may also find it cathartic to chuck things out when you've had a bad day. Personally, this is one of my favourite times to let things go.

Have a plan for letting go of unwanted stuff

Chapter Eight offers ideas on how to create a plan for donating, selling or recycling your unwanted stuff. The key to success is getting things out of your home as soon as possible.

The twelve-point decluttering plan

Now you're ready to start clearing your clutter. For the purposes of illustrating the twelve-point plan, let's say you choose to declutter and reorganise your wardrobe. The same basic approach works for all areas in your home, though.

1. Choose an area and set your goal

Once you've selected your wardrobe, your goal is to streamline your clothes so they are current season, current size, in good repair, and you wear and feel wonderful in all of them. You will save time in the mornings because you'll be able to see what you own at a glance. Your wardrobe will reflect your life, style and size today.

2. Completely empty out the area you're working on

Chances are it's been a long time since your wardrobe was anything other than jam-packed. Totally emptying the space allows you to reassess the best way to use it. Don't try and fast-forward this stage by shuffling things about in situ. I promise you will get much better, longer-lasting results by being thorough now.

Cover the bed with an old sheet to protect it. Then take all the clothes out of the wardrobe and pile them on the bed. Put any miscellaneous junk from the bottom of the wardrobe on to the floor to deal with later.

No matter how clean your home is, clutter attracts dust and dirt. Throw open windows while you are working to ease the atmosphere. Give the wardrobe a quick vacuum and make sure things are clean before putting them back.

3. One thing at a time

Handle one piece of clothing at a time. Hold each item up and ask yourself honestly, have you worn it in the last year, does it fit you and is it in good condition? Overall, does it pass the Smile Test? Do you feel a million dollars wearing it? Make quick decisions as the longer you hum and ha, the harder you'll find it to decide. You will start to become sidetracked by how much it cost, whether you had value from it, whether your partner likes it and whether you will have enough clothes left if you let it go.

Once you have determined you no longer want something, your next decision is what to do with it. Put unwanted clothes into the blue charity bag. Put clothes that have had their day into either the black rubbish bag or the recycling box. Put to one side anything you want to sell.

4. Store like with like

Clothes you choose to keep are now hung back in the wardrobe. Face all hangers the same way and categorise clothes by colour and whether they are work or leisure. Put your white work shirts together on one side and your weekend clothes on the opposite side. I love colour-coding wardrobes – it may sound a bit over the top but it is so easy to see what you own if all your jeans are side by side. The most common reaction I meet is shock when somebody realises they have 14 pairs of chinos and 11 pairs of blue denims.

Containers such as baskets, Tupperwares, decorative tins and shoe boxes will work as temporary storage solutions. Put similar items like your shoe-cleaning stuff together in a tin. If you're a frequent traveller, place flight socks, sponge bag and a copy of your travel insurance in your carry-on bag so you are ready to go.

5. Make the best use of storage space

Pack away out-of-season clothes in the loft, in under-bed drawers or in the wardrobe in your spare room. Sentimental items such as your wedding dress or the lime-green pedal pushers you loved in college can be stored elsewhere.

Now look carefully at maximizing the storage space. Is there room at the bottom of the wardrobe for a shoe rack or a small drawer unit? Make a note to upgrade mismatched hangers to more appealing ones.

6. Deal with everything you've taken out

Once you've sorted your clothes, go through all the clutter that was lurking at the bottom of the wardrobe. Why are you keeping a hammer, an atlas, a box for the hairdryer you chucked last year and a stack of old magazines in there? Junk the box and recycle the magazines. Keep a laundry basket by the door for things that need to be rehomed at the end of the session. Avoid the temptation to dart about your home with lots of individual things. It wastes energy and it's easy to get distracted. Remain focused and stay in the room you are working in.

7. Very Important Things (VITs)

The exception is if you come across your passport, cheque book or keys. American decluttering expert Cindy Glovinksy calls these VITs (Very Important Things). Put these in a safe place immediately. You do not want them slipping under a pile of clutter again. Jot down in your notebook where they are.

8. Can't decide?

Don't get in a spin if you dither over a few objects. Just put them to one side and go back to them at the end of the session. If you find you are struggling to decide about most things and starting to feel distressed, take a break. Then give yourself permission to make the best choices you can.

Perhaps you are not quite ready to let something go. If you're going to the gym three times a week and are determined to get back into your size 12 clothes, put them in the loft with the current date on and make a note in your diary to decide in six months' time. If you haven't lost the weight by then, give them away.

9. Make an action list

Jot down any outstanding jobs such as taking your blue suit to the dry-cleaners or getting your black sandals heeled. Also note anything that needs to be returned to its owner or given to a friend. Write today's date and a deadline to complete the task.

10. Finding homes for your stuff

Now take the laundry basket, with all the misplaced items you unearthed, round your home, putting things back where they belong. Return the hammer to the toolbox and put the atlas back on the bookshelf.

You will be left with miscellaneous items that have never had a proper storage home. Think of the best place to store the electric fan heater you only use when the central heating breaks down. It would be better in the hall cupboard than in the bottom of your wardrobe.

Finding new homes for things is an organic process. Experiment until you find what works best. If you tend to be absent-minded, make a note of where you are putting things.

11. Tidying up at the end of each session

At the end of each decluttering session it is crucial to allow a few minutes to tidy up. It's still your living space even if the decluttering is ongoing.

Take all rubbish bags out and put the charity bags straight into the car. Designate a temporary home – perhaps in your spare room – for things you plan to sell or give to friends or family.

12. Admire your work

Don't skip this stage! Take a minute to admire your clutter-free, beautifully organised space. If you are feeling energised, take a quick break before you tackle the next area. Perhaps you're ready to sort out that carrier bag of odd socks now! At the end of the session focus on how much you have achieved and reward yourself.

Five tips for when the going gets tough

1. Challenge clutter thoughts

As you get the dusty bread-maker out from the dark recesses of your cupboard it's easy for clutter thoughts to spring into your mind. You paid £50 for it, you're busy now but you will use it in the future, you feel guilty because you've only used it once, it's so long since you had friends over for lunch . . . and on it goes. Before you know it, you've stuck it back into the bottom of your cupboard. It'll probably be another few years before it sees the light of day again. In your heart of hearts you wish you'd never bought the thing and you won't miss it when it's gone. But . . .

So challenge those clutter thoughts. Whatever you've spent on your bread-maker, it's already gone – if you want to try to recoup some of the money, advertise it in *Loot*. Or give it to a friend who's more of a domestic goddess than you. Some things work for us and some don't. For every client I see who declutters a gadget like their bread-maker there's another who swears by it. You tried it and it wasn't for you – so let it go. You really will feel better.

2. Avoid the clutter shuffle

As we saw with the bread-maker, it's tempting to put off making a decision. In the meantime the clutter shuffle beckons. Instead of accepting that you no longer need or want something, you shuffle it off to a different part of your home. You may con yourself that you have actually dealt with it. Why do you think spare rooms, lofts, garages and sheds are so full of junk? Perhaps you've even gone one stage further and shuffled your unwanted junk off to a self-storage unit.

But at some level you will still know that this stuff belongs to you. Lofts and garages are the graveyard of clutter, where all that unwanted stuff goes to moulder and disintegrate. The space we live in costs us money for rent or mortgage. If we allow our spare room to be a dumping ground for junk, we are wasting money and the opportunity for a great home office, taking in a lodger or simply having a beautiful space for guests.

Similarly, self-storage units are expensive. They are ideal for the short term such as a house move, but ask yourself if all the junk you are storing is worth the money you are paying.

So don't shuffle the clutter – if you know in your heart of hearts you'll never use those crystal glasses or cassettes again, let them go today.

3. Never reclutter areas

Once you have cleared an area like your wardrobe, make it a priority to keep it clutter-free. In this way it will act like a beacon shining out in your cluttered home. Revisit it whenever you are feeling overwhelmed or ineffectual at clutter-clearing. Remind yourself that soon your whole home will be like this.

Mandy's husband was sceptical that she would ever change her cluttered ways and he felt depressed every night when he came home and found the living room knee-deep in the aftermath of the day's activities. Mandy was determined to prove him wrong and once she had thoroughly decluttered she spent ten minutes every evening alongside her young son putting things to rights. This gave her back her self-belief that she could regain a more organised way of life that had been swept away by living with a toddler.

4. Take breaks when it all gets too much

Decluttering involves lots of decisions and dealing with stuff you have been putting off for a long while. So you're going to reach a point where you've had enough. You can't face another thing. Cindy Glovinsky calls it 'Thing Nausea', when you start to feel queasy and overwhelmed. So take time out – have a cup of tea or go for a walk to clear your head.

Repeat positive thoughts. Say to yourself, 'I can let go of clutter.' 'I can let go of things I no longer want or need.' When you feel calmer, go back to the task and remind yourself that you will succeed by handling one thing at a time.

5. How to stay motivated over the longer term

• Don't fall into the habit of focusing on how much there is still left to do. Take pleasure from every achievement, however small. Joe was delighted with his reorganised cutlery drawer. It cheered him up every time he used it.

• Don't get too hung up on where the stuff is going. Older clients are often heartbroken that no one in the family wants to inherit treasured heirlooms. Accept that this is a consequence of increasingly affluent times plus changing tastes in interior design. If no one you know wants that bone china tea service, sell it at auction. Its new owner will cherish it and you can put the proceeds towards a holiday.

- Don't despise ten minutes' work here and there. It's amazing how much you can achieve in a few minutes' concentrated decluttering. So tackle a bookshelf or drawer next time you are waiting for the kettle to boil.
- Decluttering can be hard work, so give yourself a reward. It's vital that we take care of ourselves and recharge our batteries. Treats don't need to be 'things'. Instead, take pleasure from an experience. Enjoy a trip to the cinema, watch the world go buy as you drink a cappuccino, meet a friend for lunch, buy a bunch of flowers or sip a glass of wine in the garden.

chapter four

The Whistle-stop
Tour of the House

I t is now time to take a quick tour round your home and open the doors on individual rooms. To create clutter-free space, think about both the function and the ambience of each room.

Take a notebook and go from room to room writing down five to ten key words describing your ideal décor and the atmosphere you want to create. The colours you choose will dramatically alter the mood of the room. For example, using a white duvet cover rather than a busy patterned one brings instant calm to a bedroom.

Add words describing your current use of the room, together with any plans you have for the future. If you'd like to turn your spare room into a playroom, let your key words reflect this. Staying clutter-free is all about changing habits, so question the way things are and open the way for changes and improvements. Just because you've paid your bills on the kitchen table for the past two years doesn't mean you can't set up a desk area in the living room.

For each room I'll examine the most common pitfalls that lead to clutter, turnaround tips to banish it and the key words that I would use to describe each room. Your words may be very different as they will reflect your lifestyle and tastes.

HALLWAY

After a long day, as the door swings open, does it feel great to be home at last? Are you greeted by a welcoming oasis of space and order that takes you naturally through to your living space? Or do your spirits sink as you fight your way through heaps of schoolbags, carrier bags, sports holdalls, coats, shoes, old newspapers and unopened post? If so, you probably avert your eyes from the mess and adopt the 'drop and run' approach, adding today's stuff to the pile and moving on as quickly as you can.

Common pitfalls

Hallways are incredible clutter magnets. Yesterday there was just one pair of shoes, today it looks as though the contents of an entire shoe shop have been tipped out. Halls are often small, narrow spaces that don't lend themselves to storage. You can count yourself incredibly fortunate if have a coat cupboard or understairs storage.

Halls are also a limbo zone with things in transit – on their way out or in. The clothes back from the dry-cleaners were put on the hook for a moment and a whole month has passed. Clive had adopted the multi-bag approach to his consultancy work. His tiny hallway was festooned with bags full of work from the past six months on their way to his home office. Just to add to the clutter he also had weeks' worth of junk mail and free newspapers mixed up with his extensive collection of designer trainers.

Turnaround tips

- Visualise your key turning in the lock and opening on to clear space. Keep this vision in mind and return to it when things get out of hand.
- Only put things in transit in the hall if you are taking them out of your home next day. It's a myth that leaving something out will remind you to deal with it. If you've been used to clutter you will have a well-tuned ability to screen out things that are lying around. So make a note on your to-do list instead.
- Limit the number of coats and bags you keep out at any one time. Store the overflow in your wardrobe. Make sure that each of your children has a peg at their own height so they can hang up their jacket and bag.
- Commit to dealing with the paper that floods your hallway daily. Every day transfer it directly to your action tray, the recycling box or your filing cabinet.
- When you arrive home, keep moving and in one continuous swoop take things where they belong rather than dumping them in the hall.

Key words

Clear space, flow, lift spirits, coming home, light colours, mirror.

KITCHEN

Lifestyle programmes talk about the kitchen as the social centre and heart of the modern home. As well as for cooking and doing the laundry, kitchens are used as playrooms, for entertaining, homework, paying the bills, working from home and watching TV. If you have a large kitchen-diner or open-plan kitchen, this may well describe your home. However, there is a sharp divide between these spacious kitchens and those in modern flats and traditional homes where two is definitely a crowd. In a compact kitchen there is no room for multi-tasking.

Common pitfalls

The most common problem in kitchens, whatever their size, is way too much stuff. The British tendency to hold on to the old while buying the new is clearly highlighted here. Delving through a cutlery drawer, there is often a startling mixture of contemporary cutlery intermingled with scary rusting implements from the past few decades. Not to mention an array of old keys, screws and general flotsam that has settled in there.

Hoarding food is a basic human instinct dating back to the leaner times of our ancestors. When Paul and I cleared out his larder he had canned food from the early 1990s. Although he is only in his 40s his parents had lived through the Second World War and he shared their horror of wasting food. He was happy to eat out-of-date food, much to my consternation and against my explicit advice.

Our relationship with cooking and food is a complex one. It

goes back to childhood, family meals and celebrations. Even if we live a fast executive lifestyle, our kitchens may reflect a yearning for a different time in our lives: shelves filled with spices, glass jars full of pasta, and fridges crammed with fresh ingredients that end up rotting and being binned. Despite the proliferation of cookery programmes on TV, we are all cooking less.

It's curious that although we live in times of plenty we still seem to feel a need to stockpile supplies. Do you feel anxious if your food cupboards are not well stocked? Do you crave a large American fridge that will hold enough food so you are perpetually ready to feed the multitude?

Turnaround tips

- Streamline everything – the kitchen is the place to play the numbers game. Only keep as much as you need and use. You don't really need 15 vases, do you? Just keep a few and pass on the rest. Do the same with your cookbooks, crockery, pans, baking equipment and glasses.
- Dump anything that is chipped. It's unhygienic as bacteria can live in the cracks. A pet hate of mine is drinking out of chipped mugs.
- Keep track of your food supplies. Clear out the fridge once a week and go through cupboards monthly. Put the most recent stuff at the back of the cupboard and eat the oldest stuff first. Save money by having a frugal month and eating your way through some of your excess in the freezer or store cupboard.
- Only keep gadgets you use regularly. It's easy to be seduced by a juicer at New Year for your planned detox. By February it's lurking in the cupboard taking up a lot of space. Before

buying any new kitchen gadget ask yourself, realistically, how often you will use it. Can you get by without it? Teresa had a pancake-maker gathering dust when all she needed was to mix up some batter and use a frying pan.

- Is there a mismatch between your kitchen equipment and lifestyle? If you barely have time to grab a ready meal and pre-prepared vegetables to microwave, accept this. Stop buying lots of fresh ingredients you don't have time to cook.
- Be ruthless with dross in 'really useful drawers'. Kitchen drawers attract an incredible array of old birthday candles, corks out of wine bottles, bits of toys, free sugar packets and matchbooks from restaurants, chargers for old mobile phones, batteries and loose change. Dedicate just one drawer for useful things and junk the rest.
- Carefully define what activities go on in your kitchen and only keep things there that match it. I'd advise anyone to keep paperwork out of the kitchen. There's something depressing about a pile of papers on top of the microwave and they can easily get stained with spillages.
- Kitchens are greasy places so only put things out on display that you use regularly.
- Keep surfaces and kitchen tables as clear as possible – it looks better and it'll be easier to clean and keep hygienic. Remember, kitchen surfaces are generally for action, not for storage.
- Be inspired by innovations in kitchen design. You don't have to splash out on a deluxe fitted kitchen to benefit from looking round kitchen showrooms for storage ideas. You can often buy one-off pieces that will maximise storage in cupboards.

Key words

Clean, hygienic, functional, clear surfaces, cooking, good smells, laundry, beautiful crockery.

LIVING AREA

In Victorian times the parlour was kept strictly for best with all the expensive treasures on display to show visitors our wealth and status. How times have changed! One of the decluttering triggers for people is that their living room has descended into such chaos that they feel too ashamed to have anyone round. While I'm not suggesting we're permanently on standby with a duster in case there is a ring at the door, having a clutter-free living area will free us up to entertain or unwind in the evening.

Common pitfalls

Many activities go on in living rooms – socializing, watching TV, eating, kids playing, listening to music or the radio, playing on the computer, reading, chatting on the phone and simply relaxing. Lucy took this further – she liked to dress in the living room while she was watching TV and eating her breakfast. Unfortunately this meant that she left a trail of clothes, makeup and dressing gowns in her wake, all liberally sprinkled with crumbs. Marcus likes to exercise while he watches TV so his living room is dominated by bulky pieces of equipment. He also works from home one day a week, so office paperwork is scattered all over the sofas and chairs.

Living rooms are beset by too much furniture, too many

paintings on the walls and too many plants which crowd the space. Large collections of books, CDs, DVDs and videos, decorative china collections, numerous framed photos and oversized multi-coloured kids' toys can make this room feel oppressive.

Finally, the killer clutter factor in living rooms is usually papers – a disordered mess of glossy magazines, old newspapers, holiday brochures mixed in with letters, bills and important stuff.

Turnaround tips

- Walk around your living room and look at it with fresh eyes. Focus in turn on the décor, the furniture, the lighting, the pictures on the walls, everything. What changes would you need to make to create the room you desire?
- Chuck out any dead or ailing plants that are beyond redemption. Plants, like cut flowers, add life to a room only if they are vigorous and healthy.
- Prune your collections down to a manageable size. I know that for many people it is a criminal act to part with a book they have read. But if you're a keen reader, it's easy for your home to be overrun with books. Only add novels to your bookshelves if you will read them again. Keep current reference books grouped by category, putting gardening books and travel books together, for example.
- Use concealed storage to make the living room look less busy.
- Assess carefully whether the living room is the best spot for paperwork. If you live in a one-bedroom flat it probably is.

Invest in a screen to keep it out of sight while you are relaxing.

Key words

Socialise, read, TV, feet up, inviting, calm, luxurious, restful, comfort, welcoming, fresh flowers.

DINING AREA

The dining room used to be an integral part of every home. These days the situation is more blurred with the move to open-plan living with kitchen-diners, loft-style apartments and knocked-through living rooms. This, combined with less formal mealtimes, has meant a lot of eating is done in front of the TV or on the move.

Common pitfalls

If you do have a dining area the most common problem is cluttering up the table with general household detritus. As well as being a place to eat it is often used for school homework, working from home and other domestic projects. It had been over a year since Tina's family had eaten in theirs. Trays on the knee were the norm and having friends over for a meal had become a distant memory. Her dining-room table was serving the same function as many people's hall area – it was her drop-and-run area.

Turnaround tips

- Get a few boxes and take everything off the table. Stand back and admire the wood. Now imagine it with only a beautiful bowl of fruit or a vase full of flowers on it. That's all that needs to live on there. Give everything else a home and appropriate storage space.
- Every day, scoop up things that have drifted on to the table and keep the surface clear.
- Use it. Have a family meal or ask friends over. Enjoy having reclaimed part of your home back from the clutter.

Key words

Sociable, wood, fruit, flowers, family, chat, laughter.

BATHROOM

Bathrooms need to function at two speeds – full on and slow and relaxing. You want to speed your way out of your home in the morning with everything to hand. Yet at the end of a stressful day, you want to wind down in a luxurious bath by candlelight.

The challenge of keeping it clutter-free will rise with the number of people sharing your bathroom. The move towards ensuites means fewer people per bathroom. However, if you share with young kids or teenagers, there will be heavy demands on this small room.

Common pitfalls

The key problems in bathrooms are often caused by trying to cram too much into a small space. Beware cosmetic overload and cluttered surfaces which are hard to keep clean. Piles of damp towels and soggy magazines all over the floor will do nothing to enhance the glamour of this room.

Turnaround tips

- If your bathroom is tiny, look at making more use of the wall space. A larger bathroom cabinet, shelving, over-the-door hooks, a heated towel rail or a corner unit would increase storage.
- Put kids' bath toys in a container – either a plastic box with a lid or a mesh bag that can be hung up to drain.
- Save time with a laundry basket with separate compartments for whites, colours and a third for dry-cleaning or hand-wash items. If space is limited, hang up a drawstring laundry bag.
- Every six months clear out your bathroom cabinet and edit your beauty or grooming products – shampoos, body lotions and shaving gear. Finish off or bin all those bottles with half an inch of the contents left at the bottom. Keep your surplus products in a basket in your bedroom or spare room.
- Store frequently used cleaning products in an under-the-sink cupboard and secure with child-proof catches. Only bulk-buy toilet rolls and cleaning products if you have enough room to store them.

- Use the bin. I'm struck by how often people leave ancient newspapers, the innards of toilet rolls and empty bubble-bath bottles lying around on the floor. Nothing makes a bathroom appear more unwelcoming than this!

Key words

Getting ready, laundry, make-up, medicine, gleaming, shower to wake up, bath to unwind.

MAIN BEDROOM

My bedroom is an oasis of calm with pale walls free of pictures. I have the minimum of things out on display and see it as a place to relax and retreat to at the end of the day. Although I'm sometimes tempted to have a small TV in there, in the end I prefer to read and listen to music. That's my bliss. What is yours?

Common pitfalls

On the Clutter Tour with new clients, the first thing I look at in the bedroom is the view from the bed. It's often not a particularly pretty sight, with overspilling drawers, chairs piled high with clothes, books and papers crammed into all the corners and wardrobes stacked with old boxes and junk. How relaxing is that at the end of a busy day?

If you overcrowd your bedroom with everything but the kitchen sink, you'll be vulnerable to a moth infestation. George kept old papers, woollen blankets and gym clothing under his bed. As we pulled things out we were surrounded by flapping moths which were steadily munching their way through the lot. The dusty, fusty atmosphere was an ideal habitat for them.

Turnaround tips

- Lie on your bed for five minutes and imagine how to transform your bedroom into a relaxing retreat. Perhaps you want to emphasise luxury with more sensual fabrics and candles.
- Banish paperwork from the bedroom entirely. I prefer to keep my bedroom free of books too, apart from the one I'm currently reading. It's more relaxing that way.
- Don't leave dirty washing lying around. Put it straight into the dirty-linen basket. I prefer having mine in the bathroom, but it may work better for you in the bedroom.
- Think carefully about whether to store anything under the bed. A bed with built-in drawers is ideal for out-of-season clothing and spare bedding. Vacuum-pack these to save space. Otherwise use specialist underbed storage to keep things dust-free.
- Seriously review whether you need somewhere to sit in your bedroom. I know the theory is great, but in reality chairs, sofas and chaises longues end up cluttered with a cocktail of dirty and clean clothes. The same goes for exercise bikes or rowing machines – do you actually use them or just hang your trousers over them? It's amazing how letting go of a large piece of furniture can open up the space in a bedroom.
- Edit your wardrobe, jewellery and cosmetics every six months. Caitlin had so many clothes they were spilling out of every drawer and her wardrobe doors wouldn't shut. Getting dressed for her involved fighting her way through

her clothes to excavate an outfit every day. She says she can't believe how little time it takes to get ready now her wardrobe is streamlined and organised.

Key words

Sanctuary, naps, unwind at the end of the day, relax, calm, romance, retreat, dressing room, head space, warm and comfortable.

SPARE BEDROOM

I'm often called in when a spare room has become so clogged up with clutter that it is no longer possible to enter. Once this situation has taken hold people just lob things in to add to the pile before shutting the door and walking away. Going in there is like entering an archaeological dig – as you get deeper and deeper things from yesteryear start to emerge. I was amazed to see a bed materialise the other day. The room was so full and piled so high I had no idea it was there.

Common pitfalls

The biggest pitfall is treating this room with no respect. It is depressing and draining to live in a home where a room is overflowing with clutter. It doesn't matter if you keep the door tightly shut, it will still get you down. Don't squander the opportunity to turn this space into a functioning and welcoming part of your home.

Turnaround tips

- Dump the notion that this is a junk room. Your first step is to redefine the space from spare room to home office or guest room (or both). Remember what you first planned for the room when you moved in. I doubt you thought this would be a great room to hold all your empty cardboard boxes.
- Now set about clawing your way back to your original plans. Invite someone to stay in a couple of weeks to give yourself a deadline.
- Consider buying a sofa bed or wall bed if you want to use this room as a home office or to house your computer and home-related paperwork.
- If you don't have a loft, cellar or garage, the storage potential of your spare room becomes critical. Before storing anything in it, ask yourself, do I need to keep this? Am I simply procrastinating and putting off the moment I have to let this go? Don't hold on to things just in case. Instead, use the storage constructively for out-of-season clothing, blow-up beds and spare bedding and your tax records.

Key words

Guests, office space, storage, junk-free zone.

KIDS' ROOMS

Kids and mess are a natural pairing. Whether they are three or thirteen there will be plenty of stuff in their rooms – some of it beloved and much of it useless clutter. When working with families, I find children vary enormously in how cooperative they are in sorting things out. Young children often fill charity bags with glee but get bored quite quickly. Teenagers are curious about my work, but prefer to sort it out by themselves, usually with a friend on hand to make it more fun.

Common pitfalls

Kids suffer from the same problem as adults – they have too much stuff to fit in their rooms. If there is also inadequate storage, the floor ends up with toys, clothing and books scattered all over the place. It can be hard for them to find any room in which to play or hang out so they'll head off to the kitchen or living room and clutter that up as well.

Turnaround tips

- Involve kids in decluttering from an early age. It gets them used to the cycle of things passing through their lives. An annual car-boot sale followed by a family treat could be all it takes to start them off filling bags.
- Limit the number of toys your child is playing with at any time. Rachel has a 'three-at-a-time rule' for her four-year-old son Damian. He has to put the first three toys away before getting new ones out. It helps keep a handle on all the small parts of toys that can so easily go adrift.
- Join your local toy library, so your child can enjoy a variety of toys without having to find permanent storage for them.
- Make decluttering a game for young children – challenge them to see how quickly they can fill up a binliner.

- Keep a schoolwork box for the year's work and at the end of the year get them to go through it and keep their favourite bits for posterity.
- Help your kids by making sure all their possessions have a home so it is easy to tidy up.

Key words

Fun, colourful, easy to manage, room to play, homework, friends, sleepover, teenagers – privacy, cool, express yourself.

LOFTS AND CELLARS

Lofts and cellars provide invaluable extra storage space in your home. Unfortunately, in the vast majority of cases they are misused as dumping grounds for stuff that should never have been stored in the first place.

Common pitfalls

If you believe out of sight is out of mind, you'll shuffle things to the loft or cellar until they are full to bursting. The tendency is to fill the space haphazardly rather than organise it. As the years go by the memory of what is stored there fades.

Because it becomes such a big job, people rarely clear out these spaces unless a life trigger forces it. For most people the crisis comes when they are moving home, having a loft conversion or the cellar floods. Suddenly they are confronted with all the junk that has accumulated and needs to be dealt with urgently.

Turnaround tips

- Lofts and cellars are not holding places for junk. They are spaces for storing things you will use again one day. By all means store some memorabilia there but be discriminating and don't keep every piece of nursery equipment until you have grandchildren.
- Only when you've completed decluttering the rest of your home give your loft or cellar a blitz. Leave this as the last job if you are moving home.
- Draw up a plan of storage in the loft and make sure everything is labelled and stored in dust-proof containers. In a cellar you will have to protect against damp as well by using plastic boxes with lids.
- Remember, you do not have to fill the space. Only store meaningful stuff there. Emma has absolutely nothing in her loft and she says it gives her a feeling of lightness, having that empty space above her home.

Key words

Seasonal storage, important memories, suitcases, Christmas decorations, organised, easy to access.

OUTDOOR SPACES AND GARDENS

Yesterday I was sitting on a wall waiting for an estate agent and thinking about clutter and gardens. The front garden of the house I was about to view contained litter, an old estate agent's sign, soft drinks cans, a couple of cardboard boxes and a jungle of weeds. In other words, a lot of clutter. The first piece of junk tossed in there will act as a clutter magnet and will attract more of the same.

Common pitfalls

Clutter may not be a word we normally associate with outdoor spaces but old tools, wrecked kids' toys, rotting furniture and general jetsam all create an uncared-for look. Broken bicycles or old washing machines in the garden waiting indefinitely for a skip look dreadful.

Turnaround tips

- If you have a front garden, be vigilant about picking up any litter that blows in.
- Add a couple of pots to the front-door area and it will feel like home.
- A clutter-free garden is one that is loved and cared for, whether it is a cottage garden with its riot of colour or a Zen oasis. If gardening is not your bliss, a designer will give you advice on low-maintenance strategies.
- Get a shed. Even if space is too tight for a full-size shed there are miniature ones that will hold your garden equipment. Do keep it for functional things like tools, pots and sprays instead of letting it become a junk cubby-hole.
- Call the council to take away any bulky rubbish or hire a skip today. Why not clear out your garage at the same time?

Key words

Time out, close to nature, colour, parties, peace.

GARAGE

How many people do you know who can no longer park their car in their garage because of all the junk? Garages tend to be full of pure clutter – stuff that is broken, tired or obsolete.

Common pitfalls

Rita performed a classic clutter shuffle by packing her unwanted cookbooks into a box and then putting the box into the garage. Why did she do this? Because she feared the minute she gave them away she would have an urge to make Orkney gingerbread or something else she hasn't cooked in over a decade. So she kept the whole box 'just in case'. This kind of half-hearted decluttering is incredibly common. To successfully declutter something you actually have to let it go.

Turnaround tips

- Just as you had to stop thinking of your spare room as a junk room, stop thinking of your garage as a dumping ground. The only things that belong there are your car, bicycles, paint or other chemicals you do not want to store in the house, and seasonal stuff like the parasol for your garden table.

- Just because you have space you do not have to use every last inch. Aim instead for a well-organised garage with shelving and plenty of room to walk around.
- Beware the temporary trap – you put stuff in there while you think about hiring a skip or having a car-boot sale. Two years later things are exactly where you dumped them. Keep tabs on yourself by putting the date on anything you store.
- Have an annual spring-clean of the garage like any other room in your home.

Key words

Car, paint, tools, putting outdoor stuff away in the winter.

chapter five

The Toughest
Clutter Challenges

As I go about my work organizing people's homes I'm struck again and again by how the same areas prove to be sticking points. This chapter will explore how to regain control of these nightmare areas in your home. You are in charge of this major life-cleansing process, so always start with the clutter challenges that you personally find the most straightforward. As you reclaim each neglected area of your home, you will feel freedom and balance return to your life.

THE FLOOR

On my first visit it is sometimes a challenge actually to get through people's front doors because of the sheer volume of stuff in the hallway. Using the floor as a dumping ground is the fastest way to achieve a cluttered home. Things on the floor are going to get dirty, dusty and damaged. Stairs end up strewn with bits and bobs – either on their way up or way down, but in reality stuck in limbo for weeks on end. This is not only terrible from a clutter point of view, it is also hazardous because you may slip or fall over them.

Have a look around your home and become aware of just how much of your floor space is covered with detritus. During the Clutter Tour with clients, I look behind and under furniture to see how much stuff is lurking there. What is your particular style of floor cluttering? Do you shove things under beds, behind sofas, in the hallway, up the stairs, under your desk? Do you just drop things when you arrive home, stash things on the floor in a multitude of bags or boxes? Or are there towering piles of old newspapers and magazines everywhere?

Your task

If I'm faced with a room filled with clutter, I always start with the floor. This is a practical solution because once the floor is clear it is a lot easier to move around and work effectively. So kneel down and get sorting. If you have a huge amount at floor level it's better to put it all into cardboard boxes or plastic crates in the early stages. Then set yourself a target of tackling one box or crate a day or at least one a week until they are done. Many of the things shoved on to the floor will be homeless items without designated storage. You may need to buy more shoe storage or extra hooks for coats and bags to accommodate it all.

The future

- Piling things on the floor is one habit you need to break fast if you want to achieve a clutter-free home. Get a magazine rack for papers. Stop chucking wrapping paper and carrier bags behind the sofa. By all means buy under-bed storage for your clean bed linen but don't shove junk under there. A stair basket may solve the transit problem for your bits and pieces. But you have to use it properly! Marie bought one and used it to store the family gloves, instead of to take things up and down.

• Change your perspective. Floors are for furniture, to walk on and for kids to play on rather than a place to pile and store junk. If you are cluttering the floor you may still have too much stuff or you may need to review storage solutions.

• Particularly watch out for bad habits like dropping dirty clothing on the floor or not unpacking bags from your latest shopping trip. Keep the floor clear and you will truly create clear space in which to live.

SURFACES

Do you cover every available surface in your home with bowls, photo frames, scraps and oddments? What about the window-sills – is it a struggle to draw the curtains because of all the plants, ornaments and accumulated debris on them? If clutter has you in its grip you will relentlessly cover every last inch of your shelves, tables and kitchen surfaces with stuff. This busy and confusing look to a home feels overwhelming. It's hard to focus on anything because your eyes are drawn here, there and everywhere. Finding anything among all the confusion is a nightmare.

Your task

Pick a kitchen worktop or your dining-room table or coffee table. Ask yourself if this is really the best place to stack the kids' homework, your mail, work-related paperwork, your collection of vitamins or whatever it is that's cluttering up the surface.

Get a box and clear everything into it. Give the surface a quick clean and stand back and admire the clear space. Your task now is to empty the box and find new homes for everything you want to keep.

Isla had been struggling with clutter in her large family home for many years. It had been months since anyone had been able to eat at the kitchen table. After we cleared it she vowed to keep it that way. It was a struggle at first but soon became part of her daily routine. This table was her inspiration – every day she saw she could win the battle against clutter. It helped her to move on and tackle other areas of her home.

The future

- When it comes to displaying beautiful objects, less is more. Rather than fill every shelf with photos, group three together and leave the rest of the space clear. That way you can actually appreciate what's on display.
- Keep your eye on growing clutter piles on your surfaces. If you notice bits of Lego, coins, pens and piles of business cards appearing on the mantelpiece, take action before it becomes a major chore.

- Experiment with having some surfaces completely free of decorative objects. Try having bookshelves with nothing else on them but books and clear window-sills. This will create a much more tranquil environment in your home.

FURNITURE

Too much furniture always makes a room look cluttered. In many homes furniture seems to arrive haphazardly – we inherit some, buy some and acquire other pieces. The end result is often a mismatched hotchpotch. It's easy to tune out the furniture we live with and no longer see it. Unless you enjoy trying out new arrangements, the chances are it will remain where you first plonked it down.

The aim of a clutter-free home is to enjoy everything in it, and that includes the big stuff like the sofa and the wardrobes. Furnishing a home used to be very expensive but these days, with large superstores, it's possible to pick up furniture and accessories at a reasonable cost.

Your task

Take a mini-Clutter Tour and take a long, hard look at your furniture.

- Ask yourself, does it reflect your taste now? Maybe you are sick of your art deco look and want a more contemporary style.
- Is your furniture comfortable and functional? Does the chest of drawers have enough space for all your T-shirts and underwear?

- Do you need all the furniture in each room? Do you ever sit on the chair in your bedroom? Or do you just use it to pile your ironing on?
- Where did all the furniture come from?
- Could the arrangement of furniture be improved?
- Look at the rest of the furnishings: pictures, curtains, cushions.

The future

- Your first step is to let go of any excess furniture.
- Then experiment with moving things around to see if it opens up the space. You could use a diagram to work out what fits where. Perhaps your friends are feeling strong and will lend a hand to move things around.
- Accept that times have changed. Previous generations kept furniture for a lifetime. Now we want to update the look of our homes. So don't feel guilty if you feel it is time for a change.
- I know it's not always possible to rush out and replace major capital items like sofas and beds, so keep these on your wish list for the moment. Indulge in some window-shopping – browsing round interiors shops is always great fun. I find an hour or two spent looking at beautiful furniture and accessories uplifting and inspiring.

YOUR WARDROBE

Life is too short to wear clothes that make you feel less than fabulous. I love transforming clients' wardrobes from an overcrowded muddle into an organised space that only contains clothes they love and wear.

Does extracting an outfit from your overstuffed wardrobe feel like a chore? Do the hangers tangle together? When a piece of clothing finally emerges is it a crumpled mess? Can you barely open your drawers because of the sheer volume of underwear, exercise clothes and general stuff in there? How many of these clothes do you actually wear?

Are you stalling because you feel guilty about expensive shopping mistakes, or because you have so many clothes you've forgotten what you own? Are you sentimentally hoarding clothes that meant a lot to you once but have had their day? Does your weight fluctuate and do you have clothes in at least three different sizes?

It's estimated that we wear 20 per cent of our clothes 80 per cent of the time. If you grab the same pair of black trousers every day, don't delay any longer. Sorting out your clothes and accessories is a great mood booster.

Your task

- Don't hang on to clothes that are the wrong size for you. Fluctuating weight is a problem for both my male and female clients. Sally's wardrobe had clothes ranging from size 10 to 16. Ranjan's trousers went from waist size 30 to 36 inches. We all know how depressing it is to open your wardrobe and see all those clothes that don't fit. Every day you are feeding yourself negative messages. Keeping 'fat' clothes implies you expect to put on weight again. So donate them all today. Keeping 'thin' clothes puts pressure on you to lose weight and feel bad about your current size. If you are on a fitness regime or have just had a baby, store clothes you aspire to get back into. Otherwise let them go. You may be shocked to find this leaves a pretty basic wardrobe. Now you know where the gaps are, go and treat yourself to some fantastic clothes that really flatter you.

- Keep the labels on your new clothes until you wear them. It reminds you they are waiting for their first outing. From time to time we all make mistakes, so hang on to the receipt in case you want to return them. Most shops' returns policies allow you a few weeks to do this. If you miss this period you will still be able to sell them on more easily to a dress agency.

Laura loved to shop – when we sorted out her wardrobe she found over 100 pieces of brand-new clothing with the labels still on. Many of them she would never wear – her retail therapy had got out of hand when the stresses of her job escalated. Luckily she was able to sell most of them to an online dress agency. This was Laura's wake-up call and she was able to get a grip on her excessive shopping.

- Invest in good-quality hangers. Treat your clothes with care by upgrading your motley selection of free store hangers. Wire hangers can damage clothes, so return these to the dry-cleaners. Use wooden ones for suits and shirts. Padded hangers are ideal for delicate stuff. Only put one item of clothing on each hanger. If you put four shirts on, do you really think you'll wear the ones underneath? If space is really tight, use specialist multiple hangers for trousers or skirts.
- Let some air circulate. Your aim should be to see everything you own and for hangers to move freely up and down the

rail. Take the plastic wrapping off clothes after dry-cleaning. By allowing space in your wardrobe your clothes will stay in good shape and always be ready to wear.

• Take preventive action against moths today. Moths are still very much with us in the 21st century. I've seen many suits, carpets and precious cashmere sweaters ruined by holes. Unfortunately clutter attracts moths. They love fusty clothes, old carpets and lots of dusty stuff.

Many traditional moth treatments have been banned because the chemicals are so toxic. But don't wait until your beautiful things are destroyed. Moths don't like dry-cleaned or freshly laundered clothes or natural anti-moth repellents such as lavender, cedarwood, cinnamon, cloves or horse chestnuts. So put plenty in your wardrobe and drawers. Vitally, make sure you keep your clothing and carpets clean. If moths have really taken hold in your home, bring in a specialist firm to deal with them.

• Now you've dealt with your clothes, blitz your way through your accessories. Tackle your shoes, jewellery, sunglasses, belts, ties, scarves and bags. Only keep what you've room to store and still love wearing. Make sure everything is in really good repair. I know how hard it is to part with a beloved pair of shoes, but once they are worn out, it's time to say goodbye. If your shoe collection is taking over your home, it's time to start working the one-in, one-out principle.

The future

• Edit your wardrobe twice a year, in spring and autumn. When April comes around it's time to prepare for the spring/ summer season ahead. Pack away last season's winter clothes. Make sure everything is clean to keep moths at bay. If you haven't worn a pair of tweed trousers all winter, ask yourself why you are keeping them. Why give them valuable storage space?

Now it's time to release your summer clothes from storage. Spend an enjoyable hour or two trying them on. When you get something out after six months it's easier to be objective and see whether it still looks good.

- Avoid hoarding for the future. Only keep one or two outfits of scruffier clothes for cleaning, gardening and decorating. Also limit how much you keep for fancy dress and kids' dressing up.

  Don't fall into the vintage trap – that clothes will come back into fashion. Would you really wear a garment again in ten years' time? Be selective and only keep true classics. My favourite is a 1920s black lace dress that always looks great.

- Update your image. Once you have cleared out your wardrobe, you may feel stuck in a style rut. Why not treat yourself to an image update? Larger stores will often provide a personal shopper at no charge. An image consultant can analyse the colours that really suit you so you can break free of wearing only black.

COSMETIC AND GROOMING PRODUCTS

When I first started decluttering people's homes I was amazed at the sheer quantity of makeup, shampoo, perfume, after-shave, vitamins and grooming products each of my clients had. The cosmetic and grooming industry, backed by slick advertising campaigns, is phenomenally successful at selling us hope in a jar – those ever-changing products that promise to deliver younger skin or greater charisma. Yet there is a world of difference between the glossy ads and sticky, gungy tubes mouldering on the bathroom shelf.

As Paula said, 'I know it's crazy, because I'm an intelligent woman, but I can't help myself. When I read about Cameron Diaz's favourite beauty products, I rush out to buy them. I know I've already got too much makeup but I can't resist.'

Paula had makeup bags lurking in various handbags that hadn't been used for years. Many of the top-of-the-range products in her bathroom remained unopened or had only been used once. As we talked, she revealed it was a response to her weight struggles since the birth of her daughter. She felt cosmetics was the one area where she could treat herself.

But it's not only women – the grooming habits of men have undergone a radical change. My male clients also have bathrooms laden with lotions and hair products. Men are under increasing pressure to look young and groomed both at work and socially. Celebrity role models like David Beckham and Brad Pitt are making it more socially acceptable for men to look after themselves. A new nickname has been coined for these men – the Metrosexual; 'an urban male with a strong aesthetic sense who spends a great deal of time and money on his appearance and lifestyle'.

Your task

Your aim is to only have products out in the bathroom and in your travel and makeup bag that you are currently using, and to create storage space for the overflow products. Get a cardboard box and gather up all cosmetic and grooming products from your bathroom, chest of drawers, bedside table and bags. Now divide them into three piles:

• Anything opened that you don't like, is dried up or past its sell-by date, chuck in the bin. Get rid of grotty razors, makeup or sponge bags, combs and brushes.
• Products you like and are currently using: return these to the bathroom shelves and cabinet after giving everything a good clean including bags, brushes and all the pots and tubes. Keep one transparent makeup bag with key products that you can use in all your handbags. Similarly, keep one sponge bag in your gym bag and one in your travel bag with essential supplies.
• Unopened stuff: this includes any free gifts and samples you've acquired from goodie bags, hotel bedrooms, cosmetic counters or airlines. Ask yourself how long it will take to use ten pots of hair gel. As beauty and grooming products have a short shelf life, it makes sense to re-gift new, unopened products, or donate them to charity. Charles travelled regularly and liked to buy new aftershave on each trip. We counted eight opened bottles and eleven unopened ones.

If you have a lot of products, see if there is room to store your extras in a drawer or shelving unit in the bathroom. Keep all hair products, all bath products and all suntan and travel products together so you can find things quickly. By storing like with like you will quickly see how many of each item you have. Because she was so cluttered Paula had unknowingly bought seven of the same upmarket red lipstick.

If your bathroom is tiny, find space in a spare cupboard elsewhere for your surplus products. Store aftershave or perfume out of the light to protect the scent.

The future

- Declutter your beauty or grooming products twice a year, in spring and autumn. Check the sell-by dates on all medicines and vitamins. Unused medicines should be taken back to the pharmacy for safe disposal. Make sure you replace eye makeup every six months and keep all brushes scrupulously clean. Sarah kept getting eye infections because she had been using the same mascara for five years.
- Acquire less and always check your surplus supplies before buying more. Unless they are top of the range, why bother to take home all the toiletries from a hotel visit? Simplify your routines: if you can't remember to take handfuls of vitamins every day, buy a good multi-vitamin instead.
- If you fancy a new look, treat yourself to a session with an independent professional makeup artist. Request this for a special present. This is much better than going to a makeup counter in a store where they want to sell you their branded products.

BITS AND BOBS

My least favourite decluttering challenge is being confronted with a drawer full of miscellaneous stuff like the backs off remote controls, buttons, bits of jigsaws, unlabelled tapes, unidentified keys, cables and screws. This itsy-bitsy stuff is usually a mystery to both me and my client. Most of it is pure clutter and it's tempting to junk the lot. However, about ten per cent of it still has a function.

Your task

- Throw away anything you know belongs to defunct items like the top for your old blender. Put the rest into a container marked 'lost stuff' and give yourself a month to find the missing parts. Label and date the box. If at the end of the month something is still unidentified, chuck it out.
- Some strange hoarding instinct kicks in with keys and everyone holds on to spare sets. The problem is that over the years, as you move house, change cars, jobs and suitcases, this muddled pile grows and grows. Sorting them out can stir up all those catastrophic 'what if' fantasies. I know how scary this is because a few years ago I decluttered my bulging key tin. Any keys that remained a mystery were chucked and I'm glad to say I've never missed any of them. Use your investigative powers to update your key collection. Then label the ones you are keeping. Put a code on them so that if you lose them no one else can use or identify them.

The future

I recently bought an electric toothbrush that came with wall mountings. I'm planning to move house soon so I labelled them, added the date and put them into my DIY chest. That way I'll know what they are when I move. If I don't decide to use them, it'll be easy to identify and bin them.

- Keep all parts of a gadget like a food processor in a clear plastic container. That'll save them wandering off.
- Kid's toys have so many little bits and pieces that it's easy for

them to go adrift. Use labelled plastic containers to keep them together.

• Think twice before putting some mystery object into your 'really useful' drawer. If you don't know what it is now, what do you think will have changed in six months?

DEALING WITH SENTIMENTAL ITEMS

Sorting through sentimental memorabilia is one of the most emotionally difficult challenges. Letters, photos, birthday cards, your kids' artwork, gifts from loved ones, souvenirs from your travels, inherited things, work you've done in the past, things from your childhood all connect to powerful memories. It's common to cling to all these mementoes and find it hard to part with any of them. The problem is that as the years go by and the sheer quantity grows, sentimental objects can become a burden and not a pleasure. It may also feel as though too many keepsakes are anchoring you firmly in the past.

Decluttering is not just about filling binliners, it is also about acknowledging what is important in your life. The challenge is to be sentimental but selective. Take your time to go through your memorabilia carefully and you will find there are some things you can bear to let go. Display your favourite sentimental objects so you can appreciate them every day.

Memory box

One of your most important purchases is your memory box. This is the place where you are going to store your personal treasures, special birthday cards and childhood memorabilia. Buy the most beautiful box you can find, so you honour the memories in it. Keep it accessible, it's a place that you can visit whenever you're in a reflective or sentimental mood. After each celebration add only the most meaningful cards or holiday mementoes.

Everyone in your home should have their own memory box. When your children are small you can put in precious memories like their first pair of shoes. As they get older they can make up their own treasure troves with things they love, like favourite birthday cards or secret diaries. Let them customise the box with their own artwork.

Presents

Many people find unwanted presents one of the hardest areas to deal with. We all know what it feels like to receive tacky underwear or joke socks at Christmas. In fact a recent survey found that over a third of all Christmas presents have no value at all to the recipient. We loathe the reindeer socks yet feel it would be ungrateful to give them away. But does shoving them to the back of the drawer make you feel any better? Do you really think the person who gave you the gift would want you to feel guilty and hang on to it regardless?

A genuine gift is chosen with care and given freely with love. I believe it is important to accept the gift graciously in the spirit in which it was given. But after that it's up to you what you do with it. Forget the guilt. If it is something you will never use, give it away to charity or to someone who will enjoy it. Much better than cluttering up your home.

Ten tips for stress-free gifts

- Accept that even with the best will in the world, we all make mistakes when it comes to choosing presents. It's not easy to know exactly what will appeal even to our nearest and dearest. If you like giving surprise gifts, be philosophical if your gift is wide of the mark. Similarly, take it in your stride if someone gives you something you just don't want. I was in New York last Christmas and as the stores opened on Boxing Day, people were queuing up to exchange their gifts quite happily.

- If you're not sure what to buy someone, get a 'non-thing' present that can be used or consumed, like a good bottle of wine, an exotic bunch of flowers or an aromatherapy voucher.

- Give friends and family an idea of what you want next time you have a celebration. Maybe you love being pampered but your make-up bag is bulging. So ask for a voucher for a pedicure or facial. Or maybe you'd like your family to club together and buy you a trip in a helicopter or a day in a spa. When wedding lists first arrived in the UK I thought they were a bit cold and mechanical but now I think they are a great idea. Why not have a gift list for christening parties too?

- June's aunt gives her decorative household items every Christmas that mirror her own taste, not June's. June feels obliged to keep a pair of gaudy multi-coloured cushions at the back of the cupboard and fish them out every time her aunt visits. She fears if she doesn't have them on display her aunt will notice and be offended. So resist the temptation to inquire about your gift months after you have given it. You will be putting the recipient in an awkward position if they didn't like it.

- If money is tight, set a £10 spending limit for grown-ups at Christmas. The gifts can be just as thoughtful and your New Year credit bill will be less intimidating.
- Watch out for present-giving becoming a chore. My husband travels a lot and I used to insist that he brought me back a gift. The problem was that his busy schedule meant that he was scrabbling at the airport at the last minute and brought me back things I truly didn't want. One day in desperation he brought me back a packet of smoked fish. I was less than thrilled, so we came to a compromise that he would buy me an airport present like a pen or a novel. Now we're both happy.
- Don't feel you have to get your kids a present every time you go to the shops. Working parents often feel they have to compensate their kids with stuff because they spend less time with them. Be aware of how often you give gifts to your kids outside celebrations. One look at their rooms will tell you they have plenty of stuff. So see if you can curb compulsive gift-buying.
- If your generous friends and family members like to give you their cast-offs, remember it's OK to refuse politely. This will help stem the flow of clutter into your home.
- When it comes to presents, think quality over quantity. Choose one great gift rather than lots of tat.
- Birthdays and Christmas bring a new deluge of stuff to your home. It's crucial to let some old things go to maintain your clutter-free state. Use the quiet time between Christmas and New Year to sort out your clutter. Get your kids involved too, before the toy mountain takes over your home.

Photos

People often see photos as their most precious possession – the one thing they would save from a burning house. Photos are a direct conduit that transports you back to another time and place. Given this, you would imagine that photos would be handled with kid gloves and great respect. In reality these cherished memories are rarely treated with much care. Photos end up crammed into boxes, drawers and carrier bags where they become torn and damaged.

The core problem is the staggering quantity of photos you can acquire in a lifetime. All you need to do is take a few films every time you go on holiday or attend a wedding. Hey presto, you've got boxes and boxes of the things. Patricia had so many they reduced her to tears. As well as all the ones she'd taken herself, she had inherited the family albums from her mother.

Your task

The advent of digital cameras has revolutionised the way we store photos. But we still have to sort out the conventional photos we own. Get a crate or a cardboard box and gather together all the packs of photos you have stashed away in various hidey-holes. Collect together any complete albums, half-finished ones and empty ones. Set aside an evening to begin the sorting process.

It's time to challenge the belief that you must keep every photo even if it is blurred, unflattering, a duplicate or of someone you can't even remember. Start to think like a professional photographer and only keep the very best. I believe the purpose of photos is to remember happy times in your life. If a particular memory is making you miserable, let the photo go. Honour your memories by making up albums of your favourites. Treat yourself to the most beautiful album you can find.

Be generous with your surplus – perhaps someone else would enjoy them? Why not stick some into your Christmas cards to old friends? Is there anyone in your family who is interested in tracing family trees? Perhaps they would like to have some of your ancestral photos.

Store negatives properly. The best way is to use a professional ring-binder box.

The future

- Invest in a digital camera. It's great because you can immediately see if you've captured the moment. Otherwise you can press the delete button straight away. Store your favourites on your computer.
- If you are still using a traditional camera, thoroughly edit your snaps as soon as they are developed. Put some out on display, make a collage, put a few into your album. Have fun with them.
- Rotate the photos you keep on display. It brings a new energy and new memories into your home.
- Keep your albums accessible, so you can indulge in some nostalgia whenever you're in the mood.

Inherited things

When we lose someone dear to us, our first reaction is to hold on to the things that belonged to them as tangible reminders of their life and presence. However, after bereavement there is often time-pressure to clear a house, so people end up taking a lot of possessions back to their own homes.

Your task

As time moves on, you may want to keep only a few of the things you inherited. But you feel inhibited and disloyal. You ask yourself – is it disrespectful to give away things that belonged to someone you loved? Does it feel as though you are throwing away sacred memories? But is it honouring that person to shove things out into the garage or up into the loft? If heavy dark Victorian furniture is not to your taste, why not sell it at auction? Take a photo first, if you would like a permanent reminder. Then buy something that you truly enjoy so you can remember your loved one that way.

The future

- If you want to pass on family heirlooms to your children, limit the quantity. If they are old enough, ask them to choose special pieces they would like to inherit.
- Without being maudlin, we all need to think what we would like to happen to our possessions when we die. At an emotionally charged time like bereavement, family feuds can flare up over who inherits what. So write a clear will that specifically states who is to inherit which possessions.
- Pass heirlooms on in your lifetime. In the last years of her life my granny gave me several special pieces of jewellery which I still treasure. If you have something you don't need any more, why not let someone close to you enjoy it today?

COLLECTIONS

When you think of collections, it's probably stamps, coins, records or thimbles that spring to mind. But in reality a collection can be anything from stilettos to stashes of electronic gadgets, laptops, digital radios and your ever-expanding piles of books.

The *Oxford English Dictionary* defines 'collection' as 'A group of things collected or gathered together, e.g. literary items, specimens, works of art or fashionable clothes'.

Every collector knows the thrill of hunting down a first edition, rare vinyl or a Clarice Cliff vase. Collecting can be great fun, providing hours of pleasure. The problem starts when collections are starting to take over your home or have become a serious bone of contention with your partner.

Maggie started collecting pigs on her 21st birthday and since then she's been given soaps, crockery, towels, stationery, pictures – all adorned with pigs. It's just that in her late 30s, she's fed up with being surrounded by pigs. As your tastes change you may find, like Maggie, that you no longer feel the same about your once beloved collections.

Remember when you were a child and you had crazes for collecting bubble-gum cards, coins or dolls? At some point a new enthusiasm came along, and your old collections were forgotten. Well, the same is true as an adult – you don't need to keep your collections for ever.

Your task

- Count up all the different collections you currently have on the go. Assess how much pleasure they give you on a scale of zero to ten.
- If space is the issue, either limit the number of collections you have or the number of items in each. If you no longer play your guitars, why not sell the lot? Or you could just keep your favourite one for sentimental reasons.
- People often hold on to collections because they feel guilty about all the people who have contributed to them over the years. Recall the pleasure your shot glasses have given you and only keep the ones that pass the Smile Test. Allow yourself permission to let the rest go without feeling conscience-stricken.
- There are plenty of eager collectors out there, so maybe this is a good time to sell the lot on eBay or at auction.

Check whether your collections are giving you pleasure or status. For many people keeping an extensive library of books showcases how well educated they are. Remember, the key to a clutter-free home is only keeping things that make you happy. So don't keep anything just to impress someone else.

As an avid reader, I found editing my book collection one of the most challenging tasks I'd ever faced. Like many people, I found it hard to part with a book after I had read it, believing that you should keep every book you've ever read. In the past I held on to piles of dusty classics for just these reasons. Now I know they are in the local library when I want to read them. It took me some time to reach my current position, keeping only reference books I will use again or special novels that have really moved me and I plan to read again. Think about why you keep 'one-read' books such as thrillers or chick-lit novels. Why not pass them on to a friend who will enjoy them instead?

The future

It's easy for collecting to slip over the edge from pleasure to compulsion. Keep this in mind and enjoy wearing all your beautiful shoes. Don't be afraid to prune out your collections from time to time. After all, how else are you going to make room for this season's must-have boots?

chapter six

How to Stop Paper
Taking Over your Life

This whole chapter is dedicated to paper because it represents the single biggest clutter challenge for huge numbers of people. We live in such an information-rich age that it is normal to feel as though you are drowning in a never-ending stream of paper. Many people have a complex love-hate relationship with paper. They hoard newspapers, leaflets, ripped-out articles, money-off coupons and old water bills like gold dust. Over time this disorganised muddle starts to take over their homes and their lives. Frustration and chaos become part of the daily landscape as bills remain unpaid, time is wasted searching for a lost letter and cheques are mislaid under a pile of papers. As things get increasingly out of hand, even the thought of tackling paperwork is overwhelming. It's easier to procrastinate and leave it until tomorrow.

If this sounds like you, don't be despondent. Organizing paperwork may never set your heart aglow – but it is possible for it to become a routine part of life. New technology was supposed to eliminate the need for paper copies, but in reality we still need to hold on to essential documents like health records and mortgage information.

SIX KILLER PAPER PROBLEMS

1. Jumbled piles of paper

Piling papers is a recipe for clutter and disorder. These piles spread throughout the home – on floors, behind sofas, on hall tables and kitchen work surfaces, and even in the bathroom. As the heaps grow, important stuff like your home insurance policy is lost among the muddle of newspapers, junk mail, take-away menus and old birthday cards. Many people swear they know where things are, but every day they are wasting valuable time and energy looking for lost documents.

2. Systems not working

Some people I work with do not even have a rudimentary filing system for personal items like bank statements or bills. Others possess a filing cabinet stuffed to the gills with papers. It's just that on closer examination these go back many years. Often two decades of information is crammed in there. The whole cabinet presents a daunting picture, so people continue to leave vital papers lying around. Others have tried to create order using a hotchpotch of boxes, carrier bags and unlabelled folders. Not only does this look a mess, it doesn't function effectively either.

Organizing paperwork is not a natural ability for many people. Nor is it something we are taught at school. If you grew up in a family that is chronically disorganised, it won't be obvious how to file your documents or organise your utility bills. No one has ever modelled this behaviour to you.

3. Unopened post

I hadn't realised before I started working as a declutterer how many people find it difficult to open their post. I know people who've been taken to court because their phobia about the mail has led to unpaid bills and parking fines. They also miss out on positive stuff like dividend cheques and tax rebates.

Post comes through our letterbox six days a week and we are bombarded with an ever-increasing volume of junk mail. The longer you procrastinate about opening it, the harder it is to face. So ask yourself what the underlying problem is.

- Is it that you have no system for dealing with paper when it arrives?
- Do you find it hard to prioritise important mail that needs immediate action?
- Do you feel you have to study junk mail and circulars thoroughly?
- Is your shopping so out of hand that you are genuinely afraid to open bills and face up to the extent of your debts?

4. Scribbling on scraps of paper

A particularly ineffective habit is to write down important information such as addresses, telephone numbers and to-do lists on any piece of paper that comes to hand. These post-its, scraps of paper, travel cards and bits of torn newspaper are then scattered everywhere – in handbags, among the paper piles, in drawers and in your jacket pockets. Without a great memory and strong detective powers it's going to be hard to locate a telephone number in a hurry.

5. Pulling articles from magazines

The Sunday supplement has an article about weekend writing courses. You pull it out because this is something you'd enjoy. But then what do you do with it? Do you file it away immediately in a folder labelled Weekend Breaks? Or do you squirrel it away randomly and hope you'll be able to find it again in the future?

Eve attaches great value to her many jumbled-up boxes full of yellowing and out-of-date cuttings. There would be little chance that she could lay her hands on a particular article even if she remembered it in the first place. Yet she was determined to hold on to all her cuttings – even though it would take her weeks to read through and categorise them all. She fears that if she lets them go she will never access the information again.

In many ways this compulsive habit seems even stranger now that most of us have the internet at our command. It's easy to source material day and night. For many people having a physical reminder of the information is still much more potent than having it online.

6. Hoarding newspapers and magazines

Your living-room shelves are full of magazines and catalogues, there are stacks of newspapers in cupboards, by the side of the sofa, by your bed, in the bathroom and the spare room.

In your busy life you don't have time to plough through them all. Papers and magazines come with so many pull-outs and supplements these days that it is a physical chore just to carry them back from the shops. Let's face it, it can take all week to read every word of the weekend newspapers. But you hold on to them because you don't want to miss out on interesting articles. In the meantime you go on buying daily papers and glossy magazines every week and your unread collection keeps expanding.

GETTING STARTED

If you recognised yourself in any or indeed all of these problem areas, it's time to take control and get your life back in order.

Organise stationery supplies

The general rule is to buy storage after you've finished decluttering. However, in order to organise your papers, you need some supplies in the initial stages. Hold off on the big purchases like filing cabinets until you have a clearer picture of what size you need. Before you hit the stationery shop, collect together any supplies you already have.

You will need:
- An individual filing tray to hold paper that needs action like bills to pay or letters to answer
- Transparent document folders and labels
- Box files
- Ring-binder files
- Stationery supplies like paper clips, a hole punch, a stapler, permanent marker and a highlighter pen
- A shredder. These are available from stationery shops – get a heavy-duty one
- A notebook (or use your electronic organiser or computer for your to-do list)

- Magazine files to hold the collections you choose to keep
- Banks and building societies will usually supply folders for your statements
- A few small cardboard boxes

Tackle newspapers, magazines and brochures first

To reduce the sheer volume of paper lying around quickly, start by gathering up every newspaper and magazine in your home. You will never have time to read them all, so be ruthless. Remember that yesterday's news is today's fish and chip paper. If parting with them all at once makes you panicky, strike a deal with yourself. Recycle the unread newspapers but allow yourself one pile of magazines to go through. Stop buying any new ones until this pile is sorted. Now sort out catalogues, holiday brochures and phone books. Keep only the ones you use.

If you have muddled piles everywhere, give each paper or magazine a quick shake before getting rid of it, to ensure no important stuff has slipped in between the pages.

SETTING UP EFFECTIVE SYSTEMS

Now it's time to organise an efficient system for your paperwork and documents. Before you start, take a few minutes to review your current systems (if any), where to set up the paper epicentre in your home and to think about whose responsibility it is to deal with it.

Review your current filing system

Spend some time evaluating how your paperwork is currently stored. Ask yourself what is working well and what isn't working at all. Be honest with yourself if you do not have a clue what is in the bottom drawer of your filing cabinet.

Write down all the different areas of your home life that generate paperwork. If you run a business from home, completely separate home and business paperwork. Develop a filing system for each, even if it is just a different drawer in the filing cabinet.

Your domestic list might contain:

- Financial information – bank and building society accounts, credit and store cards, investments, pensions and tax records
- Health information
- Utility bills such as gas, electricity, water, council tax, phone and mobile phone
- Information for each of your children and pets
- Home insurance, car insurance and documents
- Mortgage or rental information
- Equipment manuals and receipts
- Very important documents such as birth certificates and passports

These papers are the essential categories of your filing system. Do you have existing files for any of them already? If not, make a labelled folder for each one.

As well as important documents you may also want to file interesting but non-essential information on local transport and facilities, holidays, recipes, and information relating to your leisure interests.

Choose the best place for your paperwork

Ideally all paperwork will be kept in one room of your home. Try to avoid the bedroom which is your sanctuary and the kitchen which is a place for cooking and socializing. If you haven't enough space for a designated study or office, use a screen or a desk that closes up, so you can still relax in your living space.

Whose responsibility is it?

If you live with a partner, ask yourself who currently organises paperwork – are there clear lines of responsibility? Often one person in a couple takes responsibility, but if not, divide up the jobs or take turns for a year at a time. Agree who pays bills and files away the car insurance. Any filing system should be easy for both of you to use. A family calendar and noticeboard can help keep everyone up to date with what's going on. A magnetic noticeboard in the kitchen is a good place to put invites, and the number of the local cab company. But update it at least once a month.

THINGS YOU CAN DO WITH A PIECE OF PAPER

You're going to handle one piece of paper at a time and allocate it to one of the following categories.

Action it

Use your action tray for anything you have to deal with like outstanding bills or letters to answer. Make a note of urgent actions in your notebook or electronically. At the end of each decluttering session, spend ten minutes catching up and paying bills or filling in forms.

Never put reading material or filing in here, otherwise it will overflow in a few days.

Once a week go through everything in your action tray and make sure that nothing has been forgotten.

Bin it

Recycle all your junk mail and old papers.

Use your new shredder to destroy confidential information and receipts. Trust me – shredding can be very addictive and soothing. It means no one can steal your documents and use them for identity theft. Daisy didn't own a shredder so she ripped up receipts and put them into a bin bag with used tea leaves.

File important documents

A filing cabinet is for current important information. Like your wardrobe, it needs regular clear-outs and updating. Each New Year I go systematically through every folder I own and have a weeding-out session. It's amazing how quickly information becomes obsolete.

If you believe that out of sight is out of mind, you will see a filing cabinet as a black hole that swallows paper never to be seen again. Don't be afraid of it. In order to make a filing system work, you need to personalise it and get familiar with your system. It doesn't have to be in alphabetical order. I put my client booking information at the front of my filing drawer because I use it the most frequently. Use labels that make sense to you. You could call a folder 'mobile phone', 'Orange' or 'Nokia', whatever has the most meaning for you.

If you have straightforward affairs you may be able to get away with using a few box files to hold your papers. You can set up one for utility bills and use transparent document folders inside – one for gas, another for electricity and one for phone. Box files are ideal for storing bulky items like equipment manuals and car documents.

If you have a filing tray or pile, you are doing something wrong. File daily as you go, so it never becomes a chore.

Store in your memory box

As you sort through papers you'll come across love letters, special birthday cards, concert tickets and wedding-day souvenirs. All these sentimental items belong in your memory box. Before you put anything in there, ask yourself if it is an important and happy memory. A Christmas card from your old neighbour probably has little significance to you, whereas a hand-drawn card from your beloved grandson is true treasure.

Archive old records

We all need to keep our tax records. I would advise everyone to talk to an accountant and to clarify exactly what records need to be kept. You could also discuss this with your local tax office.

Archive this information in your loft or an inaccessible cupboard. As you add the records for the most recent tax year, dispose of the oldest set.

You may also want to keep work from projects or courses you've attended. Review what you are storing on an annual basis. Ronnie found it liberating to let go of all the notes he'd painstakingly amassed for his PhD. All he kept was one copy of his thesis. He felt this allowed him to focus on his current career and aspirations.

Make a reading pile

Keep non-essential but potentially interesting reading material in your magazine rack or basket. If you don't ever get around to reading it, remember that life will go on all the same.

SORTING OUT THE DIFFICULT STUFF

Now you are ready to start dealing with the more intricate paperwork. Accept that sorting a huge backlog of papers is the most challenging and slowest part of decluttering. That way you won't waste any emotional energy on recriminations or wondering why it isn't finished in a couple of hours.

Matt had tried repeatedly to sort his papers but the end result was always that he shuffled things around into new piles and then lost them all over again. Take heart even if you have struggled with this in the past. Follow these procedures and you will succeed.

Begin with unopened post

Gather together all your unopened post. Note where the post ends up – is it always in the same place? Favourite places are kitchen tables and work surfaces, hall tables and drawers. But some people are more inventive: Jake flung his unopened mail behind the sofa and when I arrived there were many months' worth of dusty letters lurking there.

- Divide the envelopes into two piles, one for bills and personal mail and the other for junk mail and circulars. Note how much bigger the junk pile is.
- First tackle the junk mail. I know it's tempting to bin it unopened. However, it's sometimes hard to identify important business letters from the envelope. So open it, scan it in seconds, remove any personal details for shredding and then gleefully bin or recycle it. It does not deserve your respect.
- Now you are ready to tackle your real mail. Allocate to the action tray papers that need to be dealt with. File anything you need to keep. Recycle the rest.

Collect up all paperwork and start sorting

Get some boxes and gather up scattered paperwork from round your home. Take it all to where your filing system is, or where you plan to set one up. Settle down with a cup of tea. Have your action tray, your memory box, your recycling box, your magazine rack and your stationery supplies to hand.

If you are overwhelmed, set the kitchen timer for 15 minutes and see how much you can achieve in that time. Otherwise keep going for as long as you can. With paper, the key to success is not to get distracted and caught up in the minutiae. Don't start reading the newsletter on reflexology, stick it into your magazine rack.

The key at this stage is to make sure all similar papers are put together in a labelled folder. Once you've got all the papers relating to your car in a box file, it's much easier to streamline the contents.

If your filing cabinet is backed up with old documents, you are going to have to go through it all and bring it into the present. Deal with one folder at a time. There will probably be some that are completely out of date and can be chucked entirely.

Decide how long to keep records

If you don't run a business from home it is unlikely you will have to keep utility bills for tax records. So choose in advance whether you want to keep six months', one year's or two years' worth. Similarly, once you've checked your bank statements each month, ask yourself if you really need to keep all your domestic receipts and cheque stubs. For my home records, I file away receipts for major purchases like furniture and for anything that is still under guarantee, and I keep receipts for clothes for a few months in case they fall apart.

Sorting useful but non-essential papers

Decide which categories of information you want to keep. Buy a folder for each category and label it 'holidays' or 'health and beauty'. Spend ten minutes a day filing your cuttings. But be as ruthless as you can – chuck an unread five-year-old travel article, for example.

For your recipe folder use a highlighter pen to mark off recipes you have actually used and enjoy. Use subject dividers to separate out starters, main courses, puddings and cakes. Add the date to recipes you've never tried. Next time you weed out the folder you'll know the pea soup recipe has been languishing in there unused for two years. Isn't it time to bin it?

Storage solutions

When you're starting to see the wood for the trees, it's time to think about investing in more heavyweight storage solutions. Can you get by with a single drawer or do you need a four-drawer filing cabinet? Do you need a designated work space to deal with your paperwork? Do you need a stationery cupboard to house your box files and your envelopes and computer paper? Choose furniture that is both attractive and functional. Take measurements with you and decide whether you want a filing cabinet that fits A4 or foolscap folders.

If, like me, your idea of heaven is browsing in stationery shops, do think carefully before you buy copious supplies. Otherwise you'll just clutter up the place with empty folders and files!

WINNING THE PAPER BATTLE LONG-TERM

You are aiming for your paperwork to be an integral and stress-free part of your domestic life. Imagine how much easier your life will be when you can find any document in under a minute.

Have an annual blitz

Set aside time for going through all your paperwork once a year. Two good times to do it are New Year or when you complete your tax records. It's up to you. If you have a four-drawer filing cabinet, you could sort one out every three months. Make a note in your diary and stick to it. Think of a fantastic reward to motivate yourself. Once it becomes a regular part of your routine, you may even find it cathartic to throw away old papers.

If during the year your files are becoming too full and unwieldy you may need to subdivide them. Or make time for a quick declutter.

Work the one-in, one-out policy

As you file away this year's TV licence, chuck away the old one. If you decide to keep only a year's worth of personal bank statements, take the oldest one out and shred it each month.

Open your post every day

Always open the post in the same place in your home. The best spot is where you pay your bills and do your filing and your shredding.

Aim to open your post every day from now on. If you miss one, simply catch up the next day. Similarly, if you've been away for a while, grab a cup of coffee and set aside half an hour to catch up.

Note everything down

People can only remember so much information without becoming swamped and overwhelmed. Psychologists have discovered that we have difficulty remembering more than seven things at once.

So don't clutter up your brain and expect yourself to remember lots of things. Make notes in one place only – in a notebook, personal organiser or on your computer. It's much better to work off one list than a multi-coloured array of post-its surrounding your computer screen. Keep a daily list of urgent jobs to do as well as a master list of less pressing tasks.

Be more selective

If you don't want your home to become a shrine dedicated to paper, you're going to have to learn to be more discriminating.

Stop thinking of all paper as equally valuable. Treat vital documents like share certificates and insurance policies with respect. Store them so they are easily and quickly accessible. Lighten your attitude to non-essential stuff like old college notes or Christmas cards. Isn't it time to let these go?

Label and colour-code everything

Using a yellow box file for your health records and a blue one for your equipment manuals, for example, helps quick retrieval. Label everything so you never have to waste time diving around to work out what's in the folder. Even within a hanging file in the filing cabinet I would insert a separate labelled folder that can be brought out and then refiled.

Deal with paperwork little and often

Nathan hates paperwork – he finds it pure drudgery. As an artist he would rather focus on more creative activities. His fantasy is to hire a PA who will sort it all out for him. Until he gets the money to do this, he's successfully using the little-and-often approach to dealing with paper. Spending ten minutes a day on this is not intimidating and is helping him stay on top of things.

Just think of paperwork like any routine domestic chore. Imagine how overwhelming it would be if you only did your laundry once a month.

If you go through a particularly stressful or busy time, it's easy to let things slide. Like everyone else, I find that unless I keep on top of paperwork, I start to feel cluttered and inefficient. That's my warning sign to spend half an hour catching up before things get out of hand.

Treat newspapers and magazines as short-lived

- Only buy what you have time to read. Stop subscriptions to magazines that never make it out of the wrapper.
- Don't get hung up on having to read every word. Just read the interesting bits.
- Once a week speed round your home and gather up all newspapers, read or unread, for recycling.
- Store all magazines together in a magazine rack or basket. This makes it easy to grab one when you are going to work or on a journey.
- Pass your read glossy magazines on to friends or the local doctor's surgery.
- Limit your collections of magazines. You may have a particularly soft spot for *Vogue* or *GQ*. Buy attractive magazine files to store them in. But beware compulsive collecting. Don't be like Les, who has kept two copies of every edition of the *Radio Times* for the past decade.

Curb your magpie tendencies

Do you find it hard to walk past a leaflet rack without acquiring information on classes, places to go and new products? Do you find at least one useful article to pull out of each magazine you read? If so, you are very vulnerable to having your home overrun with paper. Stop and do a double-take before you acquire or save paper in the future. Ask yourself if the information is available anywhere else.

Create a wish-list folder

Leaflets and articles for things you aspire to but don't have the time or money for right now belong in your wish-list folder. Next time you want to reward yourself, get it out and have a browse through. I've been rushing around recently so mine is full of articles on pampering treatments.

Streamline your finances

Look carefully at your finances – do you really need all the credit cards, store cards and accounts you have? The fewer accounts you have, the less you have to deal with. Plus it's easier to keep an eye on your overall finances. Try the following to make life simpler:

- An online bank account means you can organise your finances when it suits you.
- Pay bills by direct debit.
- Allocate one place to keep all your receipts and check them off against your statement each month.
- If you find sorting out your taxes an ordeal, get a good accountant to help you.
- To reconnect with your spending, try just using cash for a week or always getting your personal money out on the same day of the week.
- Seek advice for debt management if you are a compulsive

shopper and have lost control of your finances. It is going to be tough, but the sooner you face up to this with the help of a professional the better.

Keep your desk clear

There is a growing trend to spend more time working from home. Your desk area needs to be a clear, uncluttered space that allows you to focus. Keep it free of stacks of paper, old coffee cups and little trinkets, photos and plants. If you like to personalise your desk, display only one special item and change it when the mood takes you. Work on one thing at a time and keep other current projects to hand in your action tray.

For Mark, putting files away was a low priority at the end of each day. Unfortunately this meant they were strewn all over the desk and floor, making it hard to find anything. Because it was getting him down, he agreed to take five minutes at the end of each day to clear up and put outstanding items back in his action tray or in the filing cabinet. This meant that each morning he faced a calm, organised workspace.

Don't create a nest around your desk. The floor area under and surrounding it is not a good storage solution. If you have filing and stationery drawers, use them appropriately. On a recent job in large offices in Central London, I found people were using their filing drawers more for spare shoes and sandwiches than paperwork.

Many work cultures still see a desk stacked with papers as a sign that someone is busy, highly creative and important. At home you can dismiss this myth. An organised, clear desk actually means you are going to be much more efficient.

Use new technology effectively

It's easy to get sidetracked on the internet. Instead of printing off an interesting article, use a good filing system in your 'Favourites' to store information. Think long and hard before you start printing anything off, otherwise you'll end up with another paper mini-mountain. Much better to set up a folder called 'Holidays' that you can go and visit next time you want a weekend away.

I find it's sometimes useful to print stuff off when it's associated with a particular short-term event, like a business meeting. You want a map of how to get there and the email correspondence on hand. Make a folder with this in it, and afterwards put that paper straight in the recycling or the shredder if it's confidential. Remember, it's all still stored in your computer.

Always back up any records you keep on the computer and keep them in a safe place. For instance, keep your home backups in your desk drawer at work.

You might want to think about buying a scanner to scan in articles as you come across them. Create a filing system on your computer, so that you don't just get a pile of unorganised scans sitting in your 'My Pictures' directory. Scanners aren't a universal panacea either. They are usually limited in format – most cost-effective ones can't scan anything much bigger than A4 size. But they are good for filing the equivalent of the newspaper clipping. You still have the information but you don't need the physical space to store it.

If you use an electronic organiser to manage your address book, your schedule or your to-do list, as more and more of us are doing, don't forget to back that data up too. Most organisers come with software that keeps the information on your PC and your organiser synchronised. Get into the habit of doing a synchronization on a daily basis, and make sure that data is included in your PC backup.

Keep on top of virtual clutter

Although computer clutter doesn't take up physical space in your home, it can easily clutter up your mind. The constant influx of spam into your inbox is irritating and a waste of time. You can buy anti-spam software, and many internet service providers are starting to provide spam filters in the emails they deliver to you. The do-it-yourself filters can be tricky to set up, and spammers are constantly finding new ways to circumvent them. Despite recent legislation and technological advances, managing the spam in your email remains a constant task. As with postal junk mail, you must delete all spam immediately, or it will pile up and obscure the stuff you do want to read.

Your email inbox should function in exactly the same way as your action tray for paper. Emails there are awaiting action. Once they are read they should be filed or deleted. Any potentially interesting articles or newsletters can be stored in a reading file that you can visit when you've got some spare time.

Mark had 7,823 emails in his inbox – he had no idea what most of them were about. It took him about eight solid hours to organise them into folders and have a mammoth deleting session. He was thrilled to end up with only 32 items that needed action. Within a few weeks, though, the number was back up to a few hundred, and he realised he had to manage them on a daily basis or be overwhelmed.

I have to confess that I have a very soft spot for emails. I have to restrict the number of times a day I check out my inbox, otherwise it's easy to waste a lot of time doing what I call 'busy work' – reading a newsletter on chocolate gifts rather than focusing on real work.

When it comes to deleting emails, decide how long to keep deleted items before losing them for ever. You can usually decide when the 'Deleted Items' folder is emptied – when you exit the programme, or when you go in and actually empty it. My advice is to choose to empty it on demand (not on exit). This is not an excuse for falling back into clutter habits and trying to hang on to old emails 'because they might come in useful'. Keep a maximum of one month's deleted emails in case you made a genuine mistake.

chapter seven

Life Events
that Trigger Decluttering

T here are certain major life events that make us stand back
and evaluate our lives. If you are starting a family, setting
up a business or moving in together, this new phase will be
filled with dreams of an exciting future. For others going
through traumas such as bereavement, redundancy, divorce or
ill-health, it will mean dealing with painful emotions and
coming to terms with loss and change.

As you enter any new phase in your life, your relationship
with certain possessions will shift and alter. By being honest
and letting go of what no longer fits your lifestyle you will free
yourself to shape your best possible future.

MOVING HOME

Moving home is well known to send people's stress levels
rocketing. It is one of the critical times when you have to
confront your clutter. There is no way you can continue to

turn a blind eye to all the stuff you have accumulated over the years.

This is an ideal opportunity for a new start without all that junk. Why pay money to shunt clutter from one home to another? With high housing costs in the UK, you are paying a premium for your spare room or garage. Don't squander the space by filling it up with all that stuff you'll never use again.

Start decluttering as soon as you know you're going to move. Alison phoned me just days before her planned move. She had been so paralysed with anxiety at the enormity of the task that she had been unable to sort out anything. Instead of lumping everything together in your mind, tackle one area at a time. As each cupboard is decluttered you'll lighten your load.

Visualise your new home free from clutter. Make a personal commitment not to repeat the cluttering patterns you established in your old home.

Staging your home for the market

When you are selling or letting your home, you want to present it in its best light. If you were going to a job interview, you'd be well prepared and looking immaculate. The same goes for your home – it's on show and there is a lot at stake. Homes can become so familiar that you no longer see the clutter and the unfinished DIY jobs. I've been house-hunting recently and I'm amazed, after all the TV programmes on selling your home, that people still show cluttered messes.

You need to consider how your home appears to a buyer. Ask estate agents for an honest appraisal. It's one of the times when spending a little money and effort can make an enormous difference to the speed of your sale and thousands of pounds' difference to the selling price.

Your aim in decluttering is to open up the space, show the storage off in its best light and make your home look clean, clutter-free and inviting. Professional declutterers or house doctors will be able to help you with this.

Presenting an uncluttered home

Your first task is to concentrate on what is out on show. Stand back and look at each room with a detached eye. You want your home to look lived in and loved, but not so full of photos and bits and pieces that it is hard for the viewer to imagine themselves living there. Less is more when it comes to staging your home. Fill your favourite vase with flowers and place a few beautiful objects on display. Keep kitchen surfaces as clear as possible. Place a bowl of lemons or other fruit on the worktop to make it look fresh. Bathrooms should also be minimal, with beautiful accessories like posh soap and fluffy towels – just think hotel bathrooms and you'll be in the zone.

If you sort out the key areas before putting your home on the market, you can tackle small areas during the sale. But don't stack packed boxes everywhere – this is unsightly and stops a house feeling like a home. While your home is on the market, don't start big decluttering jobs like the loft. Leave them until you have a definite moving date.

Storage is key

Viewers like to have a look at storage and will want to look inside your cupboards. Everyone needs somewhere to put things away, so showing your storage off well is a bonus.

Obviously you don't need to tackle *all* the cupboard clutter before you put your home on the market. (Hopefully no one is going to rummage through your bedside table or your underwear drawer.) Just think where you would look if you were viewing – the understairs cupboard, the cellar, the fitted kitchen and built-in wardrobes.

If your home has limited storage, don't draw attention to it by having stuff lying around everywhere. It sets off an alarm bell that says the house is too small.

Open up the flow in your home

Viewers need to be able to move freely round your home. So keep the floor clear – tidy away all newspapers, kids' toys, stacks of shoes in the hall. In fact, make sure the hall is as clutter-free as possible. After all, they say that people make up their minds about a property in the first 30 seconds.

Remove any obstacles that are blocking cupboards, doorways or light coming into the building. Fighting a huge cheese plant to get into a room doesn't win any hearts. If you are moving to a bigger property, putting the surplus furniture into storage will make your home look more spacious.

Finish DIY jobs

Unfinished DIY jobs are a kind of clutter. I went to view a house at the weekend which I'd been promised was spotless and ready to move into. The first room I saw had a large damp patch on the ceiling and the cornicing was falling down. I instantly felt the house was neglected and ruled it out.

So whether you pay a professional or do it yourself, don't let unfinished jobs stand in the way of your sale.

Cleanliness matters

Other people's grime is not enticing. So keep your home sparkling clean and smelling wonderful. Whether you put vanilla or lemon in a bowl of water in your microwave, brew some fresh coffee or heat up some part-baked bread, it will feel like home.

Packing and the actual move

A 2003 study by the Alliance and Leicester found that one of the most stressful aspects of moving is packing and unpacking. You may be tempted to get the removal firm to pack everything and take it all unsorted to your new home. If you choose this option, chances are that a few years down the line you'll end up with unopened boxes in the loft, garage and spare room. Amy had moved six years ago and still couldn't face unpacking all the stuff she'd brought with her.

As you pack, be brutally frank with yourself – would you really miss the second ironing board or Hoover? When did you last watch half the videos on your shelves? Why are you keeping singles when you no longer have a record player? Do you realistically ever plan to buy another one? Be determined that your possessions will not get the upper hand again.

Label all packing boxes with the room they are going to and a brief description of the contents. Keep essentials such as mugs and kettle to hand.

I know it's tempting to restore order as quickly as possible. But it will pay dividends if you take your time and experiment with the placement of furniture. Ask yourself if the space flows well and you are keeping access to doors and cupboards open.

Think about making the best use of storage space like cupboards and drawers.

Embark on a second phase of decluttering if you still have too much stuff or if some of your things no longer look so hot in their new setting.

Don't keep the cardboard boxes after the move – most removal companies will pick them up and reuse them, or you could take them to a council tip for recycling.

DOWNSHIFTING

Downshifting is often talked about in the media as a lifestyle choice. Moving to a smaller home so you can reduce your working hours, live in a simpler way or spend time abroad once you have retired are all positive reasons for downshifting. But for many people it is forced upon them by traumatic life events such as divorce, bereavement, redundancy or ill-health. Moving into a smaller property following a trauma means uprooting your life when you're at a low emotional ebb. You may be very attached to your current home and feel profound grief at the thought of moving away.

Whatever your reasons for downshifting, the challenge is to greatly reduce the quantity of possessions. Effectively you are editing your life and only keeping the most useful and valuable things. Think of it as condensing your possessions and keeping only the treasure.

I don't want to sound glib about this. I often work with people who are deeply distressed about the decluttering process prior to a downshifting move. But in order to take some of the emotional sting out of the process, assess the situation in very practical terms.

Set a numerical target

If you are moving from a 2,000-square-feet property into one that is approximately 1,000 square feet, aim to reduce your possessions by 50 per cent. Or if you are retiring from a four-bedroom house to a one-bedroom flat you'll need to shed 75 per cent of the things from the bedrooms.

Start with bedlinen and towels and simply count the number you need for your new home. Repeat the process with other household goods such as mugs, saucepans, glasses and kitchenware. By tackling the least emotionally charged items first you'll build up confidence to deal with special possessions like family heirlooms.

Check your furniture fits into a smaller place

Delia had crammed furniture from her old five-bedroom home into her two-bedroom flat. It felt overwhelming and cramped. Letting go of pieces that had been part of her life for 40 years was a real wrench. But in the end she decided that freeing up the space for entertaining was worth the upheaval. She was still able to keep her beloved corner cabinet and desk that she'd inherited from her father.

Assess the storage in your new home

How much built-in storage is available in your new place? If every cupboard in your old home is packed full with equipment, collections and general family flotsam, how much of it will you have space to store after your move? Consider what to do with all the stuff stored in the loft or garage if you are moving to a flat from a house.

The sooner you deal with it the better

Ideally you would only take with you what would fit comfortably into your new home. If this is too much of an emotional leap and your feelings are too raw, rent a self-storage unit for six months. This will allow you to take some time out to settle into your new home and make the break with the past.

But don't fall into the pitfall of taking everything with you and hoping against hope you'll fit it all in. Remember, one of the definitions of clutter is having too much stuff for the space you live in.

LIVING TOGETHER

Moving in together is an exciting step in your life. The last thing that you want is for clutter to destroy your domestic bliss. Not only are you merging two lots of possessions into one space, but more importantly two sets of beliefs about how you want your home to be. Is one of you a tidy minimalist and the other a lover of collections with only a fleeting acquaintance with the Hoover? Does one of you favour fifties kitsch and the other love simple white crockery? If so, how are you going to compromise and keep things harmonious?

The ideal situation would be to move into a place that is new to both of you. Often this is just not possible, so it is important that space is made for the incomer which they can personalise. Even if you can't afford a complete revamp, mark the occasion by choosing a new sofa together, or redecorating the bedroom.

Start as you mean to go on

Your first task is to streamline your joint possessions. If you've each had your own home you'll have duplicates of many household items – two kettles, two sets of pans, two sofas. Sit down and agree which ones to keep. If this causes arguments, take it in turns to decide. If you find yourself reluctant to part with anything that belongs to you, ask yourself whether you are feeling shaky about the future. Is holding on to your toaster a kind of insurance policy in case things don't work out?

Now is the time to agree on basic domestic rules – decide who is going to look after your joint finances, do the laundry, put out the rubbish and gather up the recycling. Sometimes it works better to divide up the jobs, so one of you takes responsibility for paying the bills and another for maintaining the car, for example.

Include in this discussion how you are going to keep your space clutter-free over time. If one of you is a hoarder, is there room to have some personal space to do with as you please? If one of you is an enthusiastic shopper, how are you going to stop clutter taking over your home? How often will you have blitzes? Could you jointly organise a car-boot sale once a year?

Review your storage: do you each have enough room for your clothes and to store your books, DVDs and CDs? Treat yourself to storage solutions that will maximise the space. Don't use the spare room as a dumping ground for suitcases and miscellaneous junk.

The wedding list

I think wedding lists are a great idea – at a practical level they stop you acquiring four coffee pots and more towels than you'll use in a lifetime. But there is a problem with drawing up the list. Faced with the catalogue or wandering round the department store, it's as though a mist descends. You start to crave expensive glasses in every shape and size and elaborate dinner services. You glaze over and select things you'll never use which will take up valuable space to store. Perhaps because getting married is an important rite of passage, compiling the wedding list is a strange mixture of becoming a grown-up and playing house.

This fantasy wedding list may come back to haunt you in later years when your tastes have changed or you start a family. Cathy's list was filled with delicate china which she no longer likes. Now it is banished to the cellar and only comes out when her in-laws visit. Her fantasy of hosting elaborate dinner parties never quite worked out. She prefers to keep things simple these days, especially since the birth of her daughter. She would like to sell the china but feels too guilty because it cost her relations a fortune and she requested it.

If you're merging homes or getting married again, you probably have everything you need. Don't be afraid to ask for bottles of wine or champagne, or theatre or garden tokens. Perhaps you'd prefer to sponsor an animal or name a star – let your imagination fly. It's your list – it doesn't have to be the usual household goods.

Bickering or breakdown?

Clutter can cause enormous tensions within couples. I'm often approached by people when their relationship is on the verge of breakdown. The clutter issue may be masking other underlying tensions about finances, long working hours and emotional connection. However, there is no doubt that living with someone else's mess can cause incredible stress.

Don't confuse a lack of domestic order with a lack of love. If you are naturally tidy and have no difficulty throwing things out, it may be hard for you to understand why your partner can't get on top of things. He or she may be overwhelmed with pressures of work or childcare and genuinely feel unable to tackle clutter.

Instead of criticizing, see if there is anything else you can do to help. Do you need a cleaner? Could you clear some of your old stuff and free up more storage space, or could you agree to take over the paperwork? In situations like this, working with a professional declutterer can help defuse the tension. The neutral approach of a professional means they can deal with the clutter without getting involved in who is to blame. Often *both* partners are hoarding and contributing to the muddle.

How to stop clutter becoming a bone of contention

- Resist the temptation sneakily or angrily to throw away your partner's stuff. It's not respectful and it won't work in the long term. Harry had been nagging his girlfriend for some time to curb her expenditure on shoes, which were taking over their flat. One day he snapped and threw away most of her beloved collection. Needless to say, she is now his ex-girlfriend.

• Nagging never works when trying to change the habits of a hoarder. If anything, it makes them dig their heels in harder. The person who is hoarding must accept there is a problem and decide to change. Model the benefits of decluttering by getting your own stuff sorted out. Taking the pressure and focus off may free them to do some decluttering of their own.

• Do discuss with your partner before getting a professional declutterer in to help. Sometimes I arrive at a house to find that couples have been fighting because one of them really didn't want a third party involved with their clutter. You can still get help sorting out your own stuff – just pick a time when your partner is out.

• If things are really bad, talk to a couples counsellor. They will be able to help you to see if other issues are involved as well as clutter or mess. Relate runs a variety of workshops, including one for couples who are moving in together.

GROWING FAMILY

New parents often regret not sorting out their home before the baby arrives. Afterwards time becomes so much more precious and your home has to accommodate all the toys and baby paraphernalia. So if you are planning a family or are currently expecting, make a start today. You want everything from your paperwork to your kitchen cupboards to be as easy to use as possible. This will save you time and stress when you are managing on little sleep.

Ask yourself what you have to let go of to make space. If

you plan to turn your spare room into a nursery, be ruthless with all the junk that has accumulated in there. For the best advice on preparing a nursery ask someone with several kids what baby equipment is absolutely essential. That way you'll avoid buying unnecessary stuff that will end up as clutter. Friends and family may well have equipment that they can pass on. Or borrow items like Moses baskets that you will only need for a short time. If space is really tight, investigate travel items that are collapsible and can be easily put away. Write a new baby or christening list so you only get what you need. Perhaps you'd prefer a car seat rather than dozens of cuddly toys.

It's a common complaint that kids today have so many toys. But little children don't go to the shops and buy themselves stuff. So where is it all coming from? Are we really doing them a favour by overloading them with toys and possessions? Think how overwhelmed you feel when you are surrounded by too much stuff. Rotating toys is one way of keeping things fresh and limiting the sheer volume of toys around.

If you are a hoarder or live in a disorganised muddle, your child will copy and assimilate this behaviour. That's why it's always best to start organizing your own clutter and model the behaviour you want your kids to adopt.

Useful tips for parents

Here are tips that have proved effective for the parents I have worked with.

• Encourage your children from an early age to see tidying up and putting away as part of the daily routine. You are preparing them for nursery and primary school (where tidying up is part of the playtime) as well as keeping some order in the house.

- Withstand pester power and you'll end up with less clutter. It's a normal part of childhood to like acquiring things. Young children today are under pressure from TV and their peers to look cool and to have the latest toys, clothes or mobile phone. Constant pestering can be very wearing but Paula says she finds that many of her daughter's requests for stuff run out of steam quickly as a new fad comes along. If she is still asking for a Barbie scooter after a few weeks, Paula knows it is something she really wants for her birthday.

- Only accept what you have space for. Two-year-old Jake's bedroom was overflowing with boxes of toys that well-meaning friends had brought round once their kids had outgrown them.

- Road-test DVDs by renting before buying. That way you will tell if your kids are going to watch them again and again or if they are just going to be clutter.

- Schools are an endless source of notices and forms that need filling in. Use a noticeboard or folder to keep them all together.

- Give your child their own labelled peg to hang up their coat and schoolbag at the end of each day.

- Get them into the habit of having regular bedroom blitzes and toy clear-outs. Watch out for oversentimentality on your part. When I work with families, parents often end up taking things out of the charity bags that the kids have happily filled. When they are old enough, do let them make the choices.

- Keep a memory box on the go for each of your children and add special toys, artwork and favourite books.

- If you have an au pair or nanny, make sure everyone knows where things are kept and stored. Otherwise it is easy for things to get misplaced.
- Stake your claim early on to adult space. At the end of a long, hard day you deserve to put your feet up and relax with a glass of wine, without being confronted with dozens of multi-coloured toys. So get the storage in the living room right. Don't beat yourself up about things not being perfect though. It's a family home you are living in, not a show house.

LANDMARK BIRTHDAYS

Birthdays with those big zeros on the end are inevitably a time to stop and reflect on your life. Are your life and home the way you imagined they would be? What changes do you need to make in the new decade to achieve your goals? If clutter has been creeping up on you for years, when you hit 40 it feels as though you have a mountain of stuff to deal with. Your lifestyle will have changed, so let your home and your habits reflect this.

Helen was about to turn 50 and was fed up to the back teeth with the relentless pace of her life. She worked long hours and compensated by hitting the shops for retail therapy. Her apartment was cluttered with stuff, much of it new purchases that had never made it out of the bags. She felt too ashamed of the mess to invite anyone over for dinner. She wanted to start dating again, but just walking round her bedroom was a real obstacle course. So her 50th birthday was a wake-up call to wrest back control. She started by negotiating a four-day week which allowed her time to start the decluttering blitz. As she sent numerous bags to the charity shop, she had to face up to all the money she had frittered away. But as she said, it only hurt for a minute to let things go – holding on to them and facing them every day cost much more.

DIVORCE

Going through a divorce or the break-up of a long-term relationship is a difficult and fraught time when the emotional temperature will be running very high. In the immediate aftermath your first reaction may be to destroy every last memento and photograph of your ex. Or you may feel as though you are on an endless Groundhog Day, poring over old photos, re-reading old emails, cards and text messages.

It is important to be gentle with yourself and understand that everyone going through a break-up will struggle when it comes to dividing up joint possessions. To dismantle a life and home you built together is a heart-rending experience. Deciding who gets what is synonymous for many people with lighting the touch paper. The things you bought together will have heightened symbolic significance as they hark back to happier times in the relationship. You may also feel shaky about your financial future and fear that unless you hold on to major capital items you will be unable to afford replacements. Anger about the break-up may spill over, so you end up fighting for things you do not even like. If you find this happening, try to understand your motivation. Are you simply trying to ensure you get a fair share? Or are you hoping to get even with your ex-partner by keeping certain items that are important to him or her? Clients have often said to me that they look back a few years after the divorce and wonder why they fought so hard for low-value items like cutlery or mugs. What felt like a matter of life and death at the time seems trivial now. Getting professional help from divorce mediation services can ease some of the conflict over dividing up possessions.

Once the dust has settled after a divorce there will be a period of re-adjustment to your changed status. You may find that many of the things you kept remind you too much of the old relationship. Consider whether it is time to let them go so that your home reflects your lifestyle now. Freeing yourself from your past will feel liberating and make space for new relationships in your life.

Rachel went through an acrimonious divorce which left her living with her children in the original family home. She longed to move on to somewhere new but financially this was not a practical option. Instead she decided to have a radical declutter and completely change the décor, the furniture and the whole feel of the place. She said the biggest moment of liberation came when she threw the marital bed into a skip. That was her true moment of letting go.

If you can't move home, follow Rachel's example. If money is tight, at least repaint the bedroom and get new bedding and bedlinen. Indulge your taste, now you no longer have to compromise. Window-shopping and adding things to your wish-list gives you something to look forward to.

Put sentimental memorabilia like photos and personal gifts out of sight for a while until you can decide more calmly what to keep. Rachel felt tempted to bin all the photos of her ex-husband but knew this was not fair to her two children. Instead, she kept family photos in her kids' bedrooms to limit her daily contact with them.

If you have a lot of things you can't bear to part with, yet it is too painful to have them around, put them away in the loft. Have another look in a year's time and decide what you want to keep. If having the stuff in your home is too distressing, use a small storage unit to give yourself breathing space. After a while, if you still want to destroy things go ahead and rip them up, burn them or jump up and down on them. The general rule with decluttering is to only keep things that are associated with good times in our lives.

Following a traumatic break-up or divorce it's important to sort things out at your own pace. See decluttering as an important tool to help with your post break-up recovery rather than another job to add to your to-do list.

BEREAVEMENT

After losing someone close to you it's normal to want to cushion yourself from emptiness and loss by surrounding yourself with their things. This is part of the grieving process when you want to hold on to their presence and all your shared memories, even their smell. This is a really tough time, so trust your own instincts about when you feel ready to go through your loved one's things. If you decide to tackle this on your own, make sure that you have someone on the end of the phone whom you can ring for emotional support.

In some instances practical issues may force the pace – after losing a parent or older relation you may be under time-pressure to clear and sell their home. Or financial restraints may mean you have to move on from the home you shared with your partner or spouse. Your emotional vulnerability at this time will make it particularly hard to make choices about what to keep. Renting a temporary self-storage unit will give you time to heal before making difficult decisions.

For some people, letting go of their loved one's belongings is unbearable. Bert, an old neighbour of mine, had lost his wife 20 years before yet still had all her clothes hanging in the wardrobe and her jewellery out on the dressing table. After some time has passed, if you can't bring yourself to part with anything, speak to a bereavement counsellor.

Ella had lost her husband several years before. Although she had managed to sort out many of his belongings she had been unable to deal with his books and paperwork. She felt it would be criminal to throw away his lifetime's work. As we talked it became clear that she wanted to pass it to someone who would value it and make use of it. His old college was more than happy to receive this collection. Knowing it had a good home meant that Ella was able to let go.

Put guilt aside and give yourself permission to let go of things you will not use or that have no special meaning for you. This does not mean you are dishonouring your loved one's memory or letting go of your love for them. Keep only the cherished objects that remind you of your life and times together. Pass on the rest to be enjoyed by others, or to raise some money to assist you through this new phase of your life.

Ideas that may help

• If your loved one was not specific about what should happen to their stuff, try and imagine what they would have liked to happen. If your husband was a deeply practical person, he'd probably prefer his tools to be used by his nephew, rather than languish in the garage. His clothing could be given to a charity shop whose aims he supported. Ask friends and family if there is a special memento they might like.

- Create your own rituals – Jake took a photo of his wife's blue summer dress before letting it go. He also burnt personal letters and diaries that he knew his wife would have wished to remain private.

- If your loved one suffered a long illness, let go of the unhappy memories associated with it such as the hospital notes and medical equipment.

- Make a special memory box where you keep their treasures – put in a favourite item of clothing, piece of jewellery and sympathy cards if you gain comfort from them.

- If you have to sort out the estate of older relatives, accept you can't bring everything home with you. Only keep meaningful items that bring back happy memories.

Losing someone close to you is a devastating experience and can take many years to come to terms with. Sorting out their possessions will be a significant part of your emotional journey. Be kind and compassionate to yourself throughout and use decluttering to help you through the tough process of letting go and acceptance.

STARTING A BUSINESS FROM HOME

Have you had enough of the daily grind of commuting, working long hours and office politics? Does the thought of running a business from home sound much more fulfilling? Spending more leisure time with friends and family or ditching your suits for your jeans is very appealing.

When you've done your market research and sorted out

your business plan and finances, there is another crucial area to consider – setting up an efficient home office. Barry hadn't considered this a priority when he started out as a freelance consultant. His natural tendency to procrastinate meant he was soon knee-deep in paper and files.

To avoid this happening to you, let's look at the best way of getting organised. There are upsides and downsides to working from home. The following suggestions will ensure it is a positive experience.

Create a designated work area

Ideally this would be a separate room so you can close the door when you are no longer working. Perhaps your spare room could become a combined guest room and office. But if you haven't got a spare room, think carefully about where you want to work. Your bedroom is not a good idea as it's your place to unwind and relax. Try not to work on your kitchen or dining-room table either. Use a desk or work station with a screen or shelving partition to define the space. Many contemporary work stations for home use are designed to close up at the end of the working day. Choose storage cupboards that conceal your equipment rather than open shelving. That way you get your living space back in the evenings and at weekends.

Don't underestimate the effect of a cluttered home

Now you are going to be around much more, the state of your home is going to affect you even more. You are no longer going to be able to escape the clutter and mess by going out to work. Clutter can be very oppressive, so before you officially launch your business have a thorough blitz of every last inch of your home. That way you will be more inclined to keep your office space clutter-free.

Set up effective systems for paper

If you've come from a large office environment you may never have organised a filing system. Many of my clients are highly creative and successful people who work from home. Angela, a property developer, is brilliant at making deals but less keen on concentrating on the minutiae of filing. There is no shame in getting professional help to set up some simple but effective systems. If you decide to do it yourself, follow the principles outlined in Chapter Six and always keep home and business paperwork separate.

Separate home life and work life

It's easy to get caught up in domestic matters and find yourself doing the laundry when you should be writing a press release. I like to spend twenty minutes in the morning organizing basic domestic matters before hitting my office or going out to a client. Make sure friends and family respect the fact that you're working even though you're at home. If you have young children, this will be more of a struggle. Mark remembers how when he was little he was barely able to breathe in his home when his father was writing in his study. Those days are long gone, so set clear boundaries for your nanny, au pair or partner about interruptions. Talk to other parents who work at home to see if they have any innovative ideas about managing this situation.

Decide on your hours

Even though you've broken free from the 9–5 rut, decide on a set number of working hours. Keep a log in your diary if this helps. If you have to fit in work and childcare, decide if you are happy to answer emails after the kids are in bed. If you are still at your computer at 11 p.m. most nights, it can end up feeling as though you never get away from work.

Take breaks

Working from home can be isolating – sometimes I miss the distractions and the gossip or just having someone around to discuss ideas with. When I feel as though I am going stir-crazy I go out for a walk or have a proper break. Going to networking events, having a good business advisor, taking proper time off to relax with friends – all these will help you stay energised.

Stay clutter-free

To succeed in the long term, apply the ideas and tips through-out this book to your home-office. If you need an incentive to get organised, why not invite an important client round to have a meeting at your home? There is nothing like a deadline to focus the mind.

chapter eight

Letting go of Unwanted Stuff

I am a passionate believer in letting go of excess stuff in a positive way that avoids unnecessary waste. There are other options than dumping it in black binliners headed for landfill. Let's strike a blow against the throw-away society we live in and give our unwanted things a second chance. Choose to donate, sell, recycle or regift them; that way we all win. We get the uncluttered home of our dreams and someone else gets to enjoy our overabundance.

I love the feeling of lightness I get after handing over a bag at the local charity shop. But if you're a confirmed hoarder, relinquishing things will be an unfamiliar experience. So don't worry if you feel a bit strange and wobbly at first. You are saying a final goodbye to your belongings and it's not uncommon to feel a sense of loss. Ambivalence is normal but don't let it stand in your way. It is only by actually letting go of things that you will feel a true sense of release and liberation.

In order to move on and renew our lives we all need to review regularly what we own and to part with superfluous stuff. That way you will create much-needed physical and emotional space in your life today.

CREATE AN ACTION LIST WITH DEADLINES

Before you start a major clear-out, sit down for a few minutes and clarify your plans. Now write down everything you need to do, with a timetable. This way you can get organised in advance by ordering a skip, arranging for the council to pick up an old mattress, or for a charity shop to collect. If you haven't got a car, perhaps a friend would help you out for an afternoon. Lindsey bought her flatmate dinner in exchange for her chauffeuring unwanted goods to the charity shop and the council tip.

As you're decluttering, make a note of everything to be sold, returned or regifted, and crucially, give yourself a deadline. The best day to take things out of your home is the day you declutter them. However, this is not always practical, so decide when you are taking the shoes to the dress agency or the magazines to the doctor's surgery. Keep track of your progress and feel the satisfaction of crossing off jobs as they are completed.

BE CLEAR ABOUT YOUR STRATEGY

There is no right or wrong way to pass your things on. It depends on what your goals are and how much time and energy you can devote to achieving them. If you want to raise money for a new bathroom, read the selling section for ideas. If Sunday morning lie-ins are your idea of bliss, lugging all your stuff to a car-boot sale at the crack of dawn may be your idea of a nightmare. If you can afford it, donate everything to charity. Don't feel guilty because you didn't turn your clutter into cash. Feel generous and positive about it.

Claire, a new mother, was just about to return to her high-powered job in the City. She decluttered thousands of pounds' worth of designer clothes and maternity gear. She was crystal-clear that her priority was to clear the room quickly for her live-in nanny. So she packed it all into a cab and sent it to one very lucky charity shop in Central London. That way she could concentrate on what really mattered to her – looking after her baby and helping the nanny settle in.

WATCH OUT FOR SABOTAGE

Don't subvert the decluttering process at this stage by suc-cumbing to any of the following temptations:

- **Rescuing your things** Mark just couldn't stop himself retrieving his old worn trainers from the rubbish bag. He knew they'd had their day but he couldn't bear to part with them. Lucy's recently donated china dogs were looking forlorn in the window of her local charity shop so she went in and bought them back.
- **Over-complex plans** This can delay the irrevocable mo-ment of separation. For three months, Jo's spare room had been full of bags of clothes she thought her sister Liz might want. The only problem was that Liz lives in New York and she wasn't going to see her for another five months.
- **Unrealistic plans** Jake wanted to sell comics and CDs on eBay but was waiting until he had a digital camera. Realis-

tically he couldn't afford one until he sold the stuff. So he stalled on a classic Catch 22 situation.

NEW HOMES FOR YOUR CLUTTER

All the suggestions in this chapter can be followed up in the Further Information section, which has useful contacts and ideas for passing on your unwanted stuff.

Donating

Charity shops

Giving to charity shops works on many levels. Your things will be re-used and the charity will generate much-needed funds. Plus it will make someone's day when they uncover a piece of treasure for £2.99.

I've donated to charities for years, so here are my top tips for giving.

- Find a charity whose aims you support and donate to their local shop.
- If you give something valuable do let them know – then they can get the true value for it.
- They want good-quality things they can sell, not junk. Make sure things are clean and in good condition – no books with missing pages or tatty underwear.
- Some charities offer collection, but this service is often run by volunteers and it can be a week or two before someone is available. Book your slot in advance.
- Don't leave things on the doorsteps of charity shops over-

night. Unscrupulous people really do steal them – it's not uncommon in London to see people rifling through bags in broad daylight.

- There are strict regulations on reselling electrical goods. Most charity shops don't accept them, but ask the manager as some shops can get things checked over by a qualified electrician before reselling.

- Due to space restrictions, most shops only take small items of furniture like side-tables or bathroom cabinets. But some larger charities with vans can collect bulky furniture. Soft furnishings need to meet current fire regulations. There are a number of schemes that refurbish furniture, white goods and computers, then pass them on to community organizations or people on low incomes.

- Charity shop staff and volunteers are usually a great source of local information. Even if they don't collect or take furniture or computers, they often know someone who does.

Community organizations

Local community organizations are usually short of money, so why not donate directly to them? It's always a good idea to check what they need first before turning up with a carload.

- Nurseries or toy libraries may be able to use toys and books your children have outgrown. Schools may welcome musical instruments, books and working computer equipment.

- Scrap bank projects and after school clubs are always in need of interesting bits and pieces for craft projects, like buttons, paper, fabric, pens and pencils, wool, and old cards for cutting up.

- Jane wanted her books to be enjoyed by as many people as possible so she donated them to the local library.
- Doctors' surgeries and hospital waiting rooms will welcome your glossy magazines.
- Charities that work with homeless people will accept clothes, food and other gifts. On a recent Christmas trip to New York I was impressed that in the lobby of the apartment building where I was staying there were boxes to collect donated items for homeless people. Supermarkets also had boxes to donate food. Charities in the UK like Crisis accept donations throughout the year.
- Animal sanctuaries need pet baskets, blankets, toys and cans of unopened pet food.

'Take me'

If you have something bulky, not worth much money, yet still perfectly serviceable, like a bookcase, an ironing board or a garden bench, try popping it outside your home with a notice saying 'Please take me'. Obviously you need to be responsible about this. Don't block the pavement and do dispose of the item if there are no takers. This strategy works well in urban areas. Over the years I've passed on many things this way including chairs, chests of drawers, cupboards and plant pots. In London it rarely takes more than a couple of hours before something vanishes. I've found the fastest time to date is five minutes.

Selling

Selling is a great option if you have the time, energy and enthusiasm for converting your unwanted clutter into hard cash. Recouping some of your initial investment may help you to let go more easily. Motivate yourself by deciding in advance on a treat from the proceeds – perhaps a day at a spa, some new DVDs, a family day out or a contribution towards your next holiday.

But be realistic about how much second-hand things make. Unless you have collectables, antiques or designer stuff, it's unlikely you'll make a fortune.

Local advertising

Selling the traditional way using local advertising is still effective. You can often place adverts in your local paper or *Loot* for free. Look through recent editions to help fix a price for your goods. A neatly printed postcard in the newsagent, library or coffee shop will cost little and reach local buyers. If you're selling a bulky item like a sofa bed, make it clear if you expect the buyer to collect.

Car-boot sales

Car-boot sales are ideal if you have a lot of stuff to sell in one go. Although you won't make much money from each item it will all add up on the day to a respectable sum. The drawback is storing the bags until the day of the sale. This is why it is crucial to find out when the next car-boot sale is before you start a major blitz.

Car-boot sales are not for everyone. Judy organised one and was in floods of tears seeing her once-prized possessions selling for 99p. But if you enjoy the bargaining and the buzz, it's a good day out. Sharing a stall with a friend will make the whole day more enjoyable – that way you can take it in turn to fetch the cups of tea!

At the end of the day, never bring unsold things back into your home. Take the good stuff straight to a charity shop and anything broken or unsaleable directly to the council tip.

Auctions

Auctions are best for good-quality collectables, antiques and china. Always ring up in advance to see whether the auctioneer does home visits or expects you to turn up with the item itself or a photo for valuation. Premier auction houses like Christie's and Sotheby's hold specialist sales of memorabilia, paintings and period furniture. Local auctions sell less valuable antiques and bric-a-brac. Check what commission, transportation and insurance costs they charge. They will also advise you about putting a reserve on an item so it won't sell at too low a price. Finally, confirm the date your goods will go on sale.

Second-hand shops

Selling your goods through a shop is ideal for designer or vintage clothes, baby gear or records. Check if the shop buys outright or gives a percentage after the items have sold.

- **Designer dress agencies** Sarah, a fashion journalist, wouldn't dream of wearing a coat from last winter. She funds next year's collection by selling off last season's through a designer dress agency.
- **Antique shops** If you prefer to sell your antiques to a shop, contact the Association of Art and Antique Dealers to find a reputable dealer. Never allow 'knockers' – that's people who just turn up at your door – into your home to see your valuables.

- **House clearance** If you plan to sell a lot of household goods, ask friends to recommend a reliable firm.

Selling online

The internet is a great way to sell your unwanted things. The phenomenal success of eBay, the online auction launched in 1995, opened the way for selling over the internet. eBay was originally started so Pierre Omidyar's wife could trade her collection of Pez dispensers. In the first three months of 2002, 5.6 million items were listed for sale on eBay UK alone. If you are a collector, beware of the temptation to buy more than you sell. A friend got so carried away bidding for a laptop he ended up paying more than the cost of a brand-new one. So stay focused – you are there to sell unwanted clutter, not to acquire it.

You can also sell your books and CDs on Amazon. There are online maternity and designer clothes shops. Have a search around and see what's out there.

Recycling

I'm a huge fan of recycling – I like the idea of things meta-morphosing into a new shape. As a gardener, I enjoy turning kitchen waste and paper from my shredder into compost. Once a month I go up to the council tip with a car boot full of plastic bottles, worn-out textiles, batteries, bulky garden waste and cardboard boxes. It always amazes me how much can amass in such a short time. I'm lucky that the London borough I live in has excellent weekly recycling kerbside collections. Many local councils are starting to organise collections for garden waste to turn into compost. Check out what collections are available in your area. One day they may even pick up and shred all those sad discarded Christmas trees left to languish in January.

Did you know that each year, every London household produces more than a tonne of waste? Only 9 per cent is currently recycled. This is very low in comparison to countries like Germany and Austria who recycle at least 50 per cent of their waste.

Mobile phones are surely one of the most quickly upgraded products around. Fifteen million mobile phones were replaced in the UK in 2003. Yet only one in 25 was recycled. So over 14 million have become clutter or gone into landfill with all their poisonous chemicals. It's estimated that immediately after Christmas 2003 750,000 phones were discarded.

Keith likes to keep up with the latest technology but he's also a hoarder. In drawers throughout his home, countless phones, chargers, accessories and instruction manuals were all jumbled up. He was hesitant to part with any of them because they were still functioning and might come in useful one day. Keith finally admitted he would be ashamed to be seen using an old phone – so he only kept his current phone. The rest he sent off in Body Shop freepost envelopes to be recycled and raise money for charity.

As well as all the more familiar items like glass bottles, drink cans and newspapers, there are many other things that can be reincarnated through recycling. Before you dump your computer, spectacles, cardboard, textiles, cans of paint, shoes and toner cartridges, check out Further Information for recycling ideas.

We also need to change the way we view the life-cycle of everyday things. A question for individuals, manufacturers and government is what is going to happen to this object when it is no longer needed? How is it going to be disposed of? Take plastic carrier bags, a fairly recent phenomenon introduced just 25 years ago. Did you know it can take hundreds of years for a bag to break down? Ireland has introduced a small charge for carrier bags that has cut usage by 95 per cent. I won a bet recently to see whether I could go a whole week without acquiring one. But it was much harder than I thought – a moment's inattention at the till and the bag would be whipped out. Now I try hard not to get one unless it's absolutely necessary.

Rubbish

Despite a creative approach to rehoming your surplus stuff, you will be left with some things like leaky pens, defunct kettles or broken kids' toys that are pure junk. Bag them up and make sure that all rubbish is put out at the end of each decluttering session. If you have a serious amount of junk like old mattresses or are tackling your garage, shed or loft, hire a skip. Leave anything usable on top. The chances are some eagle-eyed person will spirit it away.

Most councils will collect your bulky rubbish by arrangement. Usually there is a small charge – check how many items are included in the fee.

Your council information office should also be able to advise on safe disposal of paint, batteries (including car batteries) and chemicals. Old medicines should be returned to the pharmacist for safe disposal rather than binned.

Returning borrowed things

As you delve through long-neglected piles you'll unearth things you borrowed from friends and family years ago. Here are some of the borrowed items I've come across recently in clients' homes; library books three years overdue, a christening gown, a dinner suit, fold-up beds and much, much more. Does this ring a bell with you? Are there things you need to return?

Ben felt a hot rush of embarrassment mingled with guilt when he realised he still had his friend's power sander. He was tempted to shove it back into the cupboard rather than admit he'd held on to it for two years. But not dealing with it is a form of clutter.

Send a quick email with apologies and offer to return it. Chances are that if you've had it for a while, the lender will have forgotten about it too. If it's so long ago that you are no longer in touch with the person, give it to charity. Similarly, if you can't remember who you borrowed it from, ask around. But if there are no takers, let it go. As Shakespeare said, 'Neither a borrower nor lender be.'

Regifting

I love the concept of regifting. You simply hand on something you don't want to someone close to you. Say you get two copies of this year's bestseller for Christmas. Regift the duplicate to a friend or put it into your present box ready to be used as a birthday gift. Some people are very comfortable regifting a present they haven't bought themselves. And why not? We all have last-minute panics when we forget someone's birthday or are strapped for cash. However, if this makes you feel mean and dishonest, just offer it to your friend.

How to make regifting work

- Do keep a present box on the go. Just one box will do! If your kids live in a social whirlwind it helps to have gifts ready to hand. Unwanted presents or free gifts you get every time you walk near a cosmetic counter can go as a little extra into someone's Christmas stocking.
- If you have a bad memory, make a note of who gave you the original gift. This way you won't trigger a family feud by mistakenly giving back an expensive wedding gift.
- Nearly everyone I work with has well-meaning friends and family who are loading them down with unwanted cast-offs. Rosemary's best friend would turn up to visit with business suits, boxes of kids' toys and stacks of boot-sale finds. Don't clutter up your friends and family by pressing your unwanted stuff on to them. Ask them if they would like the stuff and don't be offended if they say no.
- Regift freely. People often prefer their excess possessions to go to someone they know rather than a stranger. But sometimes this can be an unconscious way of holding on to stuff. If you are still attached to a Victorian rocking chair you will be looking for it every time you visit your sister. Remember, once you have given it away it no longer belongs to you. It's up to the recipient whether to keep it or let it go.
- An elderly client of mine allocated a cupboard for all the special treasures she wanted to pass on. Now when she has a visitor they get to pick out a memento to take home.
- Ollie wraps up unwanted luxuries and uses them as place settings at her dinner parties.

Swapping parties

Arrange a get-together with a few friends or work colleagues over a glass of wine or a cup of coffee and ask them all to bring along a bag of stuff to swap. Then you can exchange a bottle of body lotion for a bestseller. It's a great way of getting a few treats. Have fun, but don't take things just because they are free. Ask yourself, would you give them house room if you had to pay for them?

Vicky and her friends get together once a year for a girls' night. They bring along their unwanted clothes and have fun trying them on and swapping them over.

SET UP ONGOING ROUTINES FOR GETTING STUFF OUT OF YOUR HOME

As decluttering becomes a familiar part of your life, you need to establish regular routines to get rid of surplus stuff. Don't feel you have to wait until your home is snowed under. At the bottom of my spare wardrobe I keep a large carrier bag for things going to charity. When it's full it's little effort to pop it round to the charity shop. I also keep a box of things I'm going to regift – like magazines for my mother, or books to pass on to friends.

chapter nine

Storage Solutions

S hopping for storage is the icing on the cake after all your hard work decluttering. It's creative and fun choosing stylish yet functional products and furniture for your home. Home interiors catalogues and lifestyle shops display a dazzling range and variety of storage solutions. In this chapter we are going to explore how to make storage work for your home and how to buy the best products. We'll also look at when it's a good idea to rent a temporary self-storage unit.

In Britain you are in a rare and enviable position if you live in a home with plenty of well-designed storage. One of the most common laments I hear is, 'I don't have enough storage space and cupboards for all my stuff.' Period properties with their attractive alcoves, fireplaces, nooks and crannies present a particular challenge. It doesn't get any easier either if your home is new. Recent statistics from the Royal Institute of Chartered Surveyors found that new homes today are 40 per cent smaller than those built 80 years ago. With this squeeze on space it's not surprising that generous fitted storage is often not a priority for property developers.

ORGANIZING YOUR STORAGE EFFECTIVELY

Always declutter before buying storage

It's tempting to kick-start your decluttering project with a spending spree. But if you haven't thought through the best solutions for your home, most of the storage products will end up as clutter. Wait a little until you have finished decluttering an area and then buy storage in a focused way.

Hannah, a dedicated shopper, fell into this trap. She had acquired a vast selection of storage products by browsing online and in catalogues and scouring home stores on the high street. She had been hopelessly seduced by glitzy box sets, raffia baskets, over-the-door products, under-the-bed drawers – anything that would stem the tide of clutter that was sweeping through her tiny one-bedroom flat. She hoped they would magically deliver order and serenity to her life. But once she got home she wasn't quite sure how to make the best use of them. All the empty containers were just adding to the muddle and confusion. As we worked together it became clear she had far too many storage products for the space she lived in. Luckily she still had the receipts and was able to return most of them.

Review your current storage

Think back to when you first moved into your home. Did you spend any time planning how to use the storage space? Or did you just take things out of the removal crates and shove them randomly into the nearest cupboard? Organizing efficient storage is rarely at the top of anyone's agenda in the middle of a stressful move.

So take time now to review how well your storage space is working. As always with clutter, watch out for the tell-tale sign of irritation as you struggle to get your blender out. If you think about how often and where you use an item this will clarify the optimum storage space.

Find the best place to store things

The old saying 'A place for everything and everything in its place' is as true today as ever. Everything you currently own and any new acquisitions need to be allocated their own storage space. Otherwise they will just wander lost throughout your home.

We use 20 per cent of our things 80 per cent of the time. That key 20 per cent needs to be easy to get your hands on. When planning storage, put frequently used items in the 'hotspots' and the least used ones in the 'coldspots'.

- **A hotspot** is easy to use, in an accessible place close to key activities. The shelf next to the cooker is one. Store your cooking oils, condiments and key utensils in a jar here because you'll be using them every day.
- **A coldspot** is inaccessible; it may involve getting on a stepladder, or it may not be well lit. Crawling into the understairs cupboard daily to fetch your shoes would get on anyone's nerves. It makes better sense to store infrequently used items such as Christmas decorations or DIY tools in there.

Storage Solutions

Keep VITs (Very Important Things) like keys, passport and cheque books in a safe place. A common mistake is choosing a new place for your passport every time you come back from holiday. How often have you stashed something away for safe keeping and then completely forgotten where it is? Mary has a habit of squirrelling away cash in odd places and months pass before it emerges again.

Match your storage to your daily habits. If you usually empty your trouser pockets in the bedroom, have a bowl on the chest of drawers for loose change. If you always take your i-Pod on the Tube, keep it in a drawer by the front door. Don't be afraid to experiment. My clients and I try out different solutions until we hit on the most effective one.

Store similar items together

The basic principle here is to store like with like so things are easy to find. Wrapping a birthday gift is a doddle if you keep birthday cards next to your wrapping paper, with a box of gifts close by. The aim is not to be like Monica in *Friends* but to save time and stress when you are looking for something in a hurry.

It makes sense to have all your sewing equipment in a tin so that it takes seconds to find a needle and black thread. Put the buttons and swatches from your new clothes in there too.

Keep stationery supplies like envelopes, stamps, labels, paper, spare notebooks and staples in one place. Put all your pens into an old mug or pen holder so that next time you are on the phone you won't need to search high and low for one. As a bonus, you'll see immediately what you have and you'll know when it's time to replenish your stocks.

Keep storage accessible and free-flowing

Putting things away should be easy. I'm struck by how often my clients pile up junk or place large objects like an armchair in front of cupboards so that they are rendered completely inaccessible. If you have to move things first, it's easier to fling it on the floor 'just for now' and another clutter mountain starts to grow.

Look around your home and move any obstructions to opening cupboards or drawers. It may mean having less furniture, but it will make storing and finding things so much easier.

Make sure you don't overfill cupboards and drawers. You don't want to move paper serviettes every time you go to grab a teaspoon.

Use space creatively

In an ideal world we would all optimise the space in our homes by having built-in storage that goes floor to ceiling. Our clothes would be stored in a well-designed fitted wardrobe. The least accessible shelf at the top could be used to store infrequently worn items such as evening shoes or bags. Instead of a single rail, you could maximise the space with two rails to hold all your shirts. Designated areas would hold your shoes, ties, belts and bags.

New ideas and exciting innovations in design are constantly emerging. I love the idea of stair treads that lift up to provide extra storage space or concealed storage that looks like part of the wall and swivels round to reveal a hidden cupboard.

If you want to commission built-in storage, ask friends to recommend a good carpenter. It may also be worth discussing your plans with an architect, especially if you want beautifully designed storage for your whole home. This way you will be able to take advantage of all the irregular spaces like under the stairs. Make sure you always consider lighting when building storage. It's ten times harder to find something if you are literally in the dark.

If built-in storage is not on your agenda at the moment, don't forget to use the full height of the room. A heated towel rail that goes vertically will use space much more efficiently. An attractive box on top of a cupboard can hold your treasures. Wall-mounted CD racks will save you valuable floor space.

Open shelving or concealed storage?

Unless you are scrupulously tidy, open shelving looks cluttered. Stacked towels on the bathroom shelves look immaculate in the brochure, but in reality are often a jumbled heap. Your bookshelves are higgledy-piggledy, with some books upright and some on their side. In front of the books, numerous framed photos, ornaments, piles of coins and general detritus have congregated. If you aren't one of life's naturally tidy people, you'd be better off with concealed storage. Just having cupboard doors makes a fantastic amount of difference to how uncluttered a room looks.

A truly minimalist home aims for clear, clean lines with most possessions cleverly concealed. While this is my ideal, I wouldn't go so far as having my kettle in a cupboard. After all, it is my home, not a homage to perfection.

Have only beautiful storage on display

Do you really want to lie in bed looking at tatty cardboard boxes on top of your wardrobe? You'd be amazed by how many people do just that. So treat yourself and make sure any storage on display is aesthetically pleasing. Buying coordinated storage boxes is an inexpensive and easy way to update the look of your home.

For the inside of cupboards and drawers, it's less important what storage looks like as long as it does the job. You can use old ice-cream cartons, shoe boxes, baskets, tins, anything you have to hand. But if this offends you, there are great drawer dividers out there on the market. Personally I hate to see a wardrobe that has unmatched hangers, but I'm quite happy to keep my batteries in an old Tupperware container in the kitchen drawer.

Finally, remember that any storage on display is vulnerable to dust and attracting miscellaneous clutter. So use products with lids which will keep both at bay.

Kids' storage

When you are designing and buying storage for young children, kneel down on the floor and see what the room looks like from their height. You'll get an accurate view of how easy it is to reach the clothes in the cupboard or the books on the shelf.

Use transparent boxes with easy-to-open lids for toys with lots of little parts. If you are looking for inspiration, check out how toys and books are stored at your child's nursery or primary school. Putting away is an important part of the daily school ritual and colours, picture or word labels and sturdy plastic boxes are used to make it easy.

A couple of my favourite storage ideas for kids' rooms are:

• A piece of string and pegs to display artwork when it's fresh.
• A colourful hammock for the cuddly toys children rarely play with, but like to have around.

Teenagers and clutter go hand in hand, so encourage them to choose funky, cool storage. If they've chosen it, they might even use it instead of the floor.

Rotate your possessions

Sometimes even after a major clear-out you find you've still got too many things to achieve the clear, uncluttered look you want. One answer is to rotate your belongings – use some and store the rest. Put half your toddler's toys away for a couple of months in an out-of-the-way place. Then swap them over – they'll seem so much more interesting.

Similarly, you can rotate framed photos, the vase you have on your table and even the pictures you hang on the wall. Store artist's prints behind one another in the same frame and then swap them round. Simple changes like this will keep your home looking fresh and contemporary.

Dual-function furniture

Years ago it would never have occurred to me to think about the storage potential of a piece of furniture before buying. I would simply have chosen a table because I liked the look of it. Yet a bedside table without drawers or a shelf means magazines and bits and pieces are more likely to end up strewn all over the floor.

So think dual function when you choose furniture. A coffee table with drawers can hold your DVDs. A trunk can be both a coffee table and a place to put away kids' toys at night. Integral under-bed drawers give you a place to store clean bedlinen or out-of-season clothing. A screen with shelving in the living room can partition off your computer area and hold your books at the same time. At the moment I'm coveting a small stepladder that doubles up as a contemporary stool.

To store or not to store

Before you store anything, go back to basics and ask yourself if you need to keep it. Do you have the space in your home for it? Is it going to be truly useful in the future?

Chances are that when you buy something new it comes in a bulky cardboard box. The question is, do you really need to keep the box? Indeed, why should you keep it? The reasons I usually hear are 'in case I move' or 'in case the item breaks down'. If you are moving soon or the item is under guarantee flatten the box out and put it in the loft. But if you live in a small flat, recycle it straight away. The rule is simple. Only hold on to things you have the space for.

When putting things in lofts or cellars, be sure they are protected against the elements and against moths or wildlife in general. Remember, lofts are subject to extremes of temperature so are not ideal for storing delicate china. Cellars are usually damp and so cardboard boxes stored here will end up mildewed. Use transparent plastic storage boxes with well-fitting lids instead.

REMEMBERING WHERE THINGS ARE STORED

Once you've stored things, it is crucial to be able to find them quickly without any fuss or stress. Remember the Clutter Test in the Introduction – it highlighted how much time you can squander looking for lost stuff. If you are organised, it should take under a minute to locate most things in your home. In the real world the odd thing will get away from you, but in the long term, aim for this minute rule. Just imagine what you could do with all that reclaimed time.

We all have different skills and talents. I can't tell my right hand from my left but find it easy to keep a mental map of where things are stored at home and rarely misplace anything. My husband Nick, on the other hand, finds it more difficult. He has a cursory look and then calls me to find the missing object. I call this the 'one-look panic' approach. He takes a quick look, panics and asks me rather than looking in the obvious places.

If, like Nick, you do not find it straightforward to locate things, you may fear that once something is put into a cupboard or a filing cabinet it will never emerge again. Don't worry. Implement the following ideas and you'll be able to lay your hands on things quickly.

Keep a record of where things are stored

This can be a database on the computer or a simple card index by subject. For Christmas decorations it would say 'in grey suitcase, left side of loft', or for birthday cards 'in shoe box on top shelf of spare wardrobe'. Obviously this only works if you keep the system regularly updated. Find a coded way of reminding yourself where valuable items like jewellery are stored. As you are carrying out the decluttering, make a note of where you are putting things.

Use labels

Don't clutter up your mind trying to remember everything. Label things as they arrive otherwise you will end up with drawers full of mystery items. A good example is spare buttons for new clothes. Snip off part of the label with the shop's name on, write 'blue dress, Dec 04' and put it back into the plastic bag with the button. Then put it into a tin with your other buttons. That way, on the rare occasion a button falls off, you'll be prepared.

The bane of my working life is all the attachments, cables and bits and pieces that come with every appliance. They rarely have the product name or number on, so it requires detective work to identify them. Put parts of a gizmo you rarely use but need to keep into a plastic bag with a description, or write on them with a permanent marker. Manufacturers could make all our lives easier by labelling all the individual parts of gizmos and equipment with the name of the product.

Resist the temptation
to constantly change things around

Avoid moving things around on a daily basis or you will only end up confusing yourself and everyone you live with.

Barry is an avid reader of books on organizational schemes. The more complex the storage system, the more attractive he finds it. Barry suffers from Attention Deficit Disorder, so it really isn't obvious to him how to store things. His creative brain can think of a number of equally viable solutions. It is hard for him to accept that there is no perfect scheme, only the simplest one that works for you.

Colour-code your storage

If you have a visual memory, use different colours so you can spot things easily. At a glance you know that the red box file contains all your current tax information and the tartan shortbread tin holds your shoe polish. Tina has a large family, so she colour-codes towels – this way, everyone knows at a glance which one belongs to them. Each family member even has different coloured socks – it's certainly an inventive way to get over the odd-sock problem.

STORAGE OPTIONS

Ideal storage products are both functional and beautiful. I adore my sleek stainless-steel linen basket because it has a hole in the lid and I can chuck dirty clothes in without opening it. I wish all storage products worked as well as this, but unfortunately many are still badly designed, flimsy and ineffective. So how do you confidently choose a product that is going to work for your home?

Let's take the example of shoes. Without storage, they end up in heaps in the hall, the bottom of the wardrobe, under the bed, scattered here, there and everywhere. I recently worked with a client and despite searching high and low we ended up with seven odd shoes. I still wonder where all those other shoes went.

Here are some of the options available for storing your shoes:

- Keep them in the original box – stick a photo on the end or just scribble a brief description on the box – 'pink strappy sandals' or 'brown suit shoes', for example.
- Buy transparent shoe boxes so they are easy to identify.
- Get a shoe rack that fits into the bottom of wardrobe, or one that sits out in the hall.
- Buy a cupboard designed specifically to hold shoes.
- Use a hanging canvas shoe container, either a large one with pockets that fits on the back of the door or one that hangs in your wardrobe.
- A carpenter could build you a customised shoe rack.

So which is the best? A lot of it is down to personal taste and your budget. Obviously keeping shoes in their original box is free and will protect them from dust. The downside is that all the different boxes can look unsightly. A shoe rack in the hall only works if you limit the number of pairs you store on it – otherwise it looks messy and can act as a clutter magnet.

Always check that any storage is sturdy, fits into the designated space and is suitable for the job. Choose a rack with solid slats that your shoes will not fall through. Check whether products are designed to fit men's shoes. Personally I don't like the hanging canvas containers because they squash shoes but I know a lot of people who are happy with them. You may decide to mix and match if you have a large shoe collection. Keep the more glamorous evening ones tucked away in their boxes and your everyday ones on a shoe rack close to hand. It's up to you whether you want to go one stage further and use shoe trees and wrap each individual shoe in its own protective bag.

USEFUL PRODUCTS

Before you head out the door, have a good browse through home catalogues and lifestyle magazines. Top this up with a wander round the shops. Ideally, go window-shopping first to get your eye in and see what's out there. The following suggestions will help you buy storage that really works for you. Suppliers' details are given in the Further Information section.

Measure your space and only buy for a specific purpose

Always measure the space for storage to fit into. List what you need together with the measurements and put the list into your purse or personal organiser. Don't forget to take a tape measure with you on your shopping trips. If you are buying a wall rack for your DVDs, take one with you so you can see how easy it is to slot in and out. If you are buying online or from a catalogue, double-check the measurements first.

If you own 1,000 CDs you will need enough storage for them all. Decide if you want them all stored together in your living room. Or do you want specific ones stored in different areas of your home? If you only listen to jazz in your office, you'll need a storage solution to fit your 70 jazz CDs. Or do you want to buy an i-Pod and archive the lot?

Don't get carried away with multi-buys. A lot of storage products come in threes. If you only want one, the other two will end up as clutter. It's better to buy distinctive containers for different purposes so that you come to associate the blue box with your daughter's schoolwork and the green one with your map collection.

Don't just buy storage because it looks attractive. Ask yourself what you would use that wicker basket for.

Think function

DIY superstores are a great source of reasonably priced transparent boxes with lids that will serve a number of purposes. Containers on wheels are ideal for underbed storage and for toy boxes. Good storage should always be well made and easy to use. Try out any product before buying. See how easy the lid is to get on and off or how smoothly drawers move in and out. If they stick, imagine what they will be like when they are full.

Strong cardboard banker's boxes are great for archiving things in lofts (though not in cellars).

Any unit with adjustable shelves is going to be so much more versatile for your outsize books or box files.

Maximise space

- Vacuum-pack out-of-season clothing or spare bedding. It's magical to see how much space this saves once all the air is sucked out.

- Use simple products like over-the-door hooks to add instant extra storage to a room.
- Place tiered shelving in kitchen cupboards so you can see clearly what you have in stock.
- Capture important memories with a digital camera so there are no more stacks of photos to find space for. That beautiful pasta picture your son made on his first day of nursery isn't going to last too long. Why not stick it on the fridge and take a photo of him next to it? That way you'll always have the memory.
- Get a wall-bed installed. Once it's folded neatly back into the wall you'll have the rest of the room at your disposal. They're ideal for studio flats and guest rooms that double up as home offices.
- Buy one of the new blow-up guest beds that pack away inside a small bag and take seconds to inflate with a foot pump. What a contrast to when I was a kid and putting up the camp bed was a lengthy and involved process.
- Fit two slim-line dishwashers rather than one full-size one. That way you can have one on a washing cycle and the other can still be used for your dirty dishes, rather than cluttering up the kitchen.

SELF-STORAGE UNITS

How many people do you know who are renting a self-storage unit for their excess stuff? I bet the number is surprisingly high. Lots of people I work with rent several at a time. One client had hers full of empty cardboard boxes and packing materials ready for her next move.

Ten years ago there were 30 self-storage warehouses in

Britain and now there are over 300, with new ones being built every week. So why are self-storage units proliferating everywhere? I believe they are a response to the cluttered times we live in. They were originally used as temporary solutions during a house move, or to store inherited possessions following a bereavement. Now the majority simply take up the slack from our overflowing homes.

If you are renting one, ask yourself what you are actually storing in there – is it junk or treasure? Have you taken things there because you can't face dealing with them? Or because one day you plan to own a second home in Italy, so you are holding on to your old furniture? Take a cold, hard look at how much money you are paying to store this stuff – ask yourself if it is really worth it.

Tim, a keen collector, lives alone in a four-bedroom house. His first question when I walked through the door was whether he should rent a storage unit for his numerous sewing machines. When we chatted more about this, Tim admitted he had lost interest in collecting them several years ago. Yet he feared he would live to regret it if he parted with them. A storage unit was appealing because he could postpone making an irrevocable decision. In the end he plucked up his courage and sold all the sewing machines. As far as I know, he has never regretted it and he has saved himself a fortune on rental costs.

There are some periods in your life when you do need time out from your possessions. In the heat of a divorce it may be very hard to decide what to hold on to and what to let go. Similarly, after a family bereavement it may feel too upsetting to sort out your loved one's things straight away. Self-storage allows you space to regain your strength and courage to sort through things.

But for most people self-storage is a way of holding on to things. Even if they are 20 miles away, you are still keeping your connection to them alive. So make sure you only store things you truly value and that you will use again in the near future.

chapter ten

Clutter-free forever

Congratulations. All your hard work clearing clutter has paid off. You've finally achieved the uncluttered home you always wanted. Have a celebration, invite friends round to admire the transformation. Tell them just how many binliners of stuff you gave away. Show off your cupboards with pride! You deserve to be incredibly pleased with yourself.

Now your challenge is to keep your home this way. In many ways it is like reaching your target weight or getting fit – you have to stay with it and develop and maintain new habits. It's a myth that a clutter-free home requires full-time dedication. The opposite is true. You'll achieve it with quick daily and weekly routines topped up with the occasional blitz. Don't listen to people who say tidy, organised people have dull lives. Would you prefer to spend your time looking for lost stuff or enjoying yourself? I know which I'd go for!

So let's look at the sure-fire tips that will keep you motivated and strategies that have worked for 'reformed clutterers'.

CLUTTER-FREE STRATEGIES THAT WORK

Do it straight away

It's strange, but once you put off the simplest task it starts to feel difficult and overwhelming. Do things at once and life is much easier. If it takes less than a minute then do it straight away.

60-second sort-its

- Chuck the empty bottle into the recycling box instead of leaving it on the kitchen counter.
- Add a contact to your address book rather than leave the details on a post-it.
- Handle things once – put the batteries into your really useful drawer immediately. Otherwise they'll soon be lost under a pile of clutter.
- Hang your clothes up at night. Make sure the dirty-linen basket is convenient so that you can put your clothes straight in rather than heaping them on the floor or on a chair.
- Always put VITs (Very Important Things) such as your passport or your keys back in the same place.
- If you come across something that is broken or used up, like dried-out nail varnish, bin it at once.
- Once you've finished reading the thriller put it straight into the bag for charity.

Katy travels regularly with her job. In the past, rather than unpack her suitcase she would buy a new one. She ended up with 13 different ones filled with clothes, half-read books, business cards and miscellaneous junk. Now she only has one overnight bag and one suitcase. 'I unpack as soon as I get home. I'm amazed it only takes about five minutes. I can't believe I used to get in such a state about it.'

Create regular routines

Psychologists have discovered that it only takes six weeks of repetition to turn a one-off action into a normal part of your daily routine. When you are first forming a habit it can seem like hard work but you will be amazed that the longer you do it, the easier and more natural it will become. After six weeks the routines will be second nature.

Daily routines

An odd five minutes here and there will keep chaos and clutter at bay. To work well, routines have got to fit in with your lifestyle and timetable.

- Get a laundry basket and collect up everything that is out of place and return it to its home.
- Get your kids to have regular pick-up time before bath or story time. Make it fun by doing it to music or using a timer.
- Open your post daily and immediately recycle or bin junk mail.
- Clear your desk at the end of each day. File papers you've finished with. Scoop up current work and put it into your action tray. It feels fantastic to walk into a clear space next morning.

Weekly routines

Until weekly routines become automatic, make a note in your diary to remind yourself of them.

- Gather up all newspapers (read or unread) and put them into the recycling box.
- Clear out your handbag or briefcase. Who knows, you might find a £20 note or some forgotten gem in there.
- Take on one small decluttering project such as sorting out your baby's pyjamas or discarding out-of-date material from your holiday folder. Little and often means that you will never again be faced with a clutter mountain.
- Go through your action tray and to-do list and make sure you're on top of all those niggling household jobs. Whether it's picking up the dry-cleaning, buying your sister a birthday present or renewing your cat's pet insurance, getting organised will make your life flow more smoothly.
- Do a Clutter Tour at speed and check out if clutter is accumulating anywhere in your home. Keep a sharp eye on clutter hotspots like the hall, kitchen surfaces and the floor. Think of those mysterious piles of junk that appear on the corner of city streets. It all started with one dumped mattress. Similarly, the first magazine dropped on to the bedroom floor will act as a clutter magnet for other stuff.

Take action if old habits are starting to resurface

It can be discouraging to find piles of junk creeping back. Look out for these warning signs: you are starting to lose things, feeling overwhelmed and irritated with your surroundings. After a hectic week, newspapers are stacked high on the floor, your dining-room table is drowning in clutter and you haven't a clue what's in your fridge.

Don't waste energy beating yourself up. No one is perfect. Instead, take an hour out to catch up before things get out of hand. Just handle one thing at a time and you will soon have restored order.

Blitz at least once a year

It's traditional to have a good clear-out in spring as the daylight returns and there's a surge of new life and energy. New Year, after the excesses of Christmas, is also a great time to have a decluttering blitz. Mark out time for blitzing on the calendar and stick to it. Mary and her daughter Jess have toy clear-outs twice a year, once after Christmas and once after Jess's birthday in June.

Aim to go through every cupboard, drawer and cubby-hole annually. I particularly like Sandra Felton's method of starting at the front door and working your way round your home. You look at and sort everything in a room before moving on to the next one.

Or you could choose to revisit one room a month for a thorough declutter and keep on top of things that way.

One-in, One-out

Every time you bring something new into your home, let a similar item go. If you buy a new alarm clock, give away the old one. This maintains the balance between what is coming into your home and what is going out. Putting an item into the garage, loft or a storage unit doesn't count. It still belongs to you and will have to be dealt with at some point in the future.

Before you buy something new, be clear what it is replacing. This will save you money as you may realise you don't actually need a new alarm clock at all!

Use it or lose it!

The general rule to apply to your functional possessions is only to keep things that you have used in the last year. Obviously there are a few exceptions to this like a special evening dress or your ski equipment. But for the majority of stuff, it applies. It's easy for things to slip from usage without you actually realizing it. The foot-massage bath was a bit of a palaver to use, so for the past two years it's been stuck under the bed and completely neglected.

If you balk at the thought of letting something go, set yourself a deadline to use it again. Either you will find renewed pleasure from it or will realise why you stopped using it in the first place. Then it will be much easier to part company with it.

Trust yourself

Stay tuned into your gut reactions so you can easily recognise when something has become clutter. Every time you take out the denim shirt you used to wear at weekends you change your mind and put it straight back into the wardrobe. This is a clue that you no longer feel good in it or maybe you associate it with your last relationship and it brings back painful memories. Either way there is no point in overanalysing this – the time has come to say goodbye. Our feelings about our possessions are ever-changing and shifting, so don't be surprised when something you loved suddenly doesn't feel right any more. If you trust your instincts it will be easier to keep your home clutter-free on an ongoing basis.

Change your mindset

Instead of expecting to keep possessions for ever, enjoy and use your things. When my granny died she had drawers full of untouched little luxuries she had stashed away for best. I came across a purse I had given her still with its little note inside saying, 'Don't keep this for best, Granny'. How many things are you keeping for special occasions that you could revel in today? Release your cashmere jumper from its tissue paper and luxuriate in its softness.

Take pleasure from the flow of things through your life. Let go of that unloved orange jug gathering dust on your shelf. Someone else will give it a good home and treasure it. This will make space for something you love looking at or you could simply enjoy the open space instead.

Adjust your self-image

When Julie finally gave up smoking after many years she found one of the biggest challenges was to think of herself as a non-smoker. Old habits like seeking out the smoking section of the restaurant were hard to break. You too will have to adjust your self-image to match your new clutter-free and organised home. You are no longer a hoarder, a squirrel, a magpie, a clutterbug, a packrat or however else you saw yourself. It will take time to acclimatise, so be patient with yourself. I still have a good look if I pass a skip even though it has been many years since I carried anything away. A little part of my self-image is still a magpie!

Review your shopping habits

People are shocked when they find I love shopping. As a minimalist and a professional declutterer my goal is to enjoy my home and I still like acquiring beautiful things I will use. I choose quality over quantity and go shopping once in a while rather than daily.

Yet we all have days when we need to make an impulse buy, to treat ourselves to something frivolous. This only becomes a problem if you become addicted to the buying high, to the rituals and trappings of shopping – the wrapping in tissue paper, the glossy carrier bag, the cosseting of the shop assistants.

If this path is leading you to a cluttered home and over-stretched finances, ask yourself before you hand over your cash or credit card:

• Can you afford it?
• Do you have space for it?
• Do you need it and will you use it?
• Does it have the wow factor?
• How much enjoyment will you get from it?

- Are you buying for emotional reasons?
- Do you need to own this? Could you borrow or hire it instead?
- Realistically, how soon will it become clutter?

If you ask yourself these questions and are still not sure, take time out and have a cup of coffee. After 20 minutes come back and have another look and decide if you want to buy it. If you remain unsure, sleep on it, and if it's right for you it will call you back. This will help you minimise shopping mistakes.

Shopping tips

- Trust your own judgement. If your partner or friends encourage you to buy stuff you don't really love, try shopping on your own. Don't settle for clothes that are just OK – find something you feel fantastic in.
- The size of your home will determine what you can buy. It's no use buying juicers, bread-makers, espresso machines and every gadget going if your kitchen is the size of a postage stamp. They'll just end up shoved in the corner of your spare room gathering dust.
- If time is tight, do your weekly food shop on the internet.
- If compulsive overspending is a problem, set yourself a weekly budget and only use cash for a month. Or if you buy yourself cosmetics every lunchtime, leave your purse behind and window-shop.
- Don't con yourself that shopping you do online, via catalogues or the TV shopping channels somehow doesn't count. The stuff will still arrive at your home and so will the bills!
- Stop buying duplicates. Lucy bought two identical toasters

because last time hers blew up it took her a week to buy a new one. Now the spare one is gathering dust on top of her kitchen cupboards. Don't prepare for the worst-case scenario as it just leads to clutter. After all, living without toast for a week is hardly an emergency.

Streamline your supplies

If you've been shopping like there is no tomorrow you've probably acquired large stockpiles. With 18 bubble baths, you don't need to look at that section of the supermarket or chemist. Not buying bubble bath will save more money than a three-for-two special offer.

• Limit the number of similar products you have on the go at once. For example, have only two kinds of shampoo out in your bathroom. This will save time as making choices is a lot easier. As you finish one, chuck the empty bottle away and fish out a new one from your stash.
• Reduce the number of spare items you store. Do you really need to have ten extra furniture polishes? Once you've reduced your stockpile, in future only keep a maximum of two spares.
• Always use a list when shopping for food and household goods. Print out a list with commonly used items and stick it on the fridge. You could use your internet shopping list for this. As you open the last jar of furniture polish, highlight it on the list. In this way you'll never run out and you don't need to keep huge supplies.

Beware bargains

The more stuff you bring into your home every year, the more time and effort you will need to engage in the battle against clutter. You only have to observe all the tat that shops shift in the sales to understand how susceptible we are to a bargain. Do not be automatically seduced by something that is free, on special offer or that a friend is giving away.

There is a cost to bargains and free stuff – you need to incorporate them into your home and find a place to store them. Remember, it is hardly a good deal if you will never use it. So think carefully before you accept or bring into your home any irresistible bargains that may well turn out to be pointless clutter.

Simple living

The simple living movement has been growing in both Britain and the USA. It challenges the way we live today – our endless round on the hamster-wheel of work and consumption. It looks for alternatives to cope with the relentless pressure to buy more and more stuff, the ever-expanding choices available and the rapid product proliferation.

Simple living is about improving the quality of life by loosening the ties to our over-materialistic society. Don't confuse it with living in a cabin without electricity or TV and weaving your own clothes. It is about questioning our insatiable need for new and expensive stuff. To illuminate whether something is really worth it to you, calculate how many hours you had to work to earn the money for it. Only you know if a pair of new shoes equates to a hard day's work!

The central question is, do you actually need this object that you are about to acquire? Will it really make your life any better? Would you rather spend the money on a weekend break instead? Personally I find this approach very helpful. Yes, I would still like a plasma TV, but I no longer feel driven to buy excess things even if they have a transitory appeal.

Say no to storing other people's junk

Again and again I've seen clients' homes overrun with bulky and unattractive stuff like cardboard boxes, bed bases or sporting equipment that they are storing for a friend or family member. The usual scenario is that this temporary situation has somehow become semi-permanent.

It's enough of a challenge to deal with your own clutter, let alone stuff belonging to people you don't even live with. So ask the person to take it away and give them a deadline. In the future politely refuse to store things for others – that is what self-storage units are for.

If your adult children have their own homes, ask them to collect the things they want to keep. That way you can finally have the office space or guest room you always wanted!

Make decluttering fun

Deprivation doesn't work. If you try to live on cabbage soup it won't be long before you're craving chocolate biscuits. To succeed at staying clutter-free, set yourself decluttering challenges to liven up the process. That way you'll enjoy yourself and keep motivated.

- See how long it takes you to fill a large carrier bag or binliner with things for the charity shop. I've seen kids fill a binliner in less than five minutes.
- Decide this month that you are going to declutter one item a day for a week, then two items a day the following week, and so on until your home is clear.
- Weigh bags as they leave your home. A great way to shed those excess pounds. Your home really will be lighter!
- Play a memory game with yourself. Did you ever play that party game where there are lots of different objects on a tray and you get a quick look then have to write down as many as possible? Without looking, note down everything you think is in the hall cupboard. See how accurate you are. Once you've decluttered and re-organised it, play the game again a few days later. You should know exactly what is in each cupboard in your home or you're still going to feel cluttered.
- Count your collections – Alice was shocked to find she had 118 novelty teapots. Put away your least favourite pieces in an unwieldy collection and if you don't miss them let them go. Aim to get it back to a more manageable number and then work the one-in, one-out policy.
- Roll a dice every day for a week. If you throw a five, your mission for the day is to hunt out five things you no longer want.
- Set yourself a day when you buy nothing but essentials such as food and travel. Join in National No Shopping Day in November.
- Subscribe to *www.nomoreclutter.co.uk*'s free newsletter which has lots of tips and challenges for staying clutter-free.

LIVING THE UNCLUTTERED LIFE

I've enjoyed sharing my passion for an uncluttered way of life with you. People tell me every day how decluttering has made their lives so much better. I wish you continued success and enjoyment of your decluttering journey. I'd love to hear your stories, so visit *nomoreclutter.co.uk* and tell me about your struggles and your triumphs.

Living clutter-free continues to be a positive and life-affirming experience for me. I love the lighter, easier way I live these days, liberated from the burden of stuff. I truly believe that whatever our individual purpose and goals in life, none of us was put on this planet to acquire and amass material possessions. At the end of the day, even our treasured possessions are not as important as our well-being, our relationships, our talents and our dreams.

Further Information

Many British people feel slightly shamefaced about bringing in a professional to help them declutter their stuff and get organised. It is still a relatively new phenomenon to pay for help with clutter in the UK, though professional organisers are well established in the USA. There is a variety of titles for them, such as declutterers, clutter consultants and house doctors who specialise in moving home.

Often my clients don't tell their friends, family or even their partners about my visits. Why is there such a stigma? Lucy felt her highly organised partner saw her clutter as a sign of laziness and something she could easily sort out herself if she put her mind to it. I would dispute this – many of my clients are very successful in other areas of their lives, but they have struggled repeatedly for years to get on top of their clutter and get organised. Remember, clutter is not a moral issue – previous generations simply did not have to deal with the same volume of possessions as we do.

As we've seen in this book, decluttering is a complex and profound process. For most of you the insights and help I've given will be all you need to get you going and keep you on the right track. However, there may be times when you need extra help, support and advice – in times of trauma such as bereavement, if you are a busy overloaded professional or full-time parent, when you are up against a deadline like moving house, or when you hit your particular sticking point like sorting out your paperwork or sentimental collections.

Finding the right person

It's vital that you trust the person helping you as the thought of a stranger going through your things can be intimidating. A professional declutterer should offer a calm, impartial expertise combined with a non-judgemental and sensitive approach. The bottom line is, it's your home and your belongings. Only you know what things mean to you, how often you use them and whether they still have a place in your life. I always work alongside my clients because I don't know the meaning and stories behind the things they own. My job is not just to help people let things go but also to help them recognise and value their special treasures.

Check out what is included in the service, such as after-care support or details of charities which collect. You have the right to expect the service to be confidential but do confirm this when booking an appointment.

Visit *www.apdo-uk.co.uk* – The Association for Professional Declutterers and Organisers UK – for more details of declutterers working in your area.

DIRECTORY

Clutter help online

The following is just a small selection of the vast range of websites on decluttering. At present most of the sites are based in the USA. Simply type 'clutter' into the search engines and check out what is available.

www.nomoreclutter.co.uk   My website has a wealth of information to help you on your way. Register for a free monthly newsletter, check out the monthly tip or send a question to the Clutter Clinic.

www.clutterersanonymous.net   follows the 12-step approach and has a quiz to work out if you are a clutterer. Their spiritual approach to overcoming clutter sees hoarding as a manifestation of deeper problems.

www.messies.com   is an active website with online support groups and useful tips.

www.flylady.net   sends out regular tips to help you fly in your battle against clutter.

Extreme hoarding

For severe problems with hoarding speak to your GP in the first instance. There may be an underlying medical condition such as Obsessive Compulsive Disorder (OCD), Attention Deficit Disorder (ADD) or depression. Treatments such as behaviour therapy can be helpful.

www.addiss.co.uk   The national ADD information and support service.

www.ocdaction.org.uk   National organization offering advice and support for people experiencing OCD.

Support organizations

www.crusebereavementcare.org.uk   Contact CRUSE for help following bereavement. National helpline: 0870 167 1677.

www.relate.org.uk   Relate offers help, counselling and workshops if clutter is causing a problem in your relationship.

www.bacp.co.uk   The British Association of Counselling and Psychotherapy has a list of qualified therapists and counsellors.

www.nationaldebtline.co.uk   offers help if your compulsive shopping has led to financial problems. Freephone: 0808 808 4000.

Donating

www.charityshops.org.uk and click on 'Find a Charity Shop'.
www.charitychoice.co.uk has a directory of charities if you want to
  donate directly to a community group.

Selling

www.yell.co.uk is a great source of secondhand shops.
www.ebay.co.uk The online auction site.
www.amazon.co.uk for selling unwanted books and CDs.
www.carbootcalendar.com lists car boot sales in the UK.

Antiques

For advice on selling antiques and for reputable dealers:

www.lapada.co.uk The Association of Art and Antique Dealers.
www.bada.org The British Antique Dealers' Association.
www.bbc.co.uk/antiques For general information on antiques and the
  best way to sell them.

Recycling

There are many organizations which can recycle and re-use
your unwanted things.

www.recycle-more.co.uk for general recycling information.
www.vao.org.uk You can send your old spectacles to Vision Aid
  Overseas, but do check with your local optician first because many
  collect instore.
www.childrensscrapstore.co.uk Re-use all sorts for children's play
  activities.
www.computersforcharity.org.uk will recondition your old PC and
  give it to a charity.
www.frn.org.uk The Furniture Reuse Network can help pass on your
  unwanted furniture and appliances to people on low incomes.

Mobile phones are recycled by numerous organizations to raise money for charity, including Oxfam, the Body Shop, Crisis, Orange and *www.matrixphones.com*

Storage solutions

You are spoilt for choice when it comes to storage. Department stores such as John Lewis or DIY superstores have a wide range of products.

www.lakelandlimited.co.uk for vacuum packs, anti-moth products, over-the-door hooks and much more.
www.theholdingcompany.co.uk Stylish storage you will enjoy using.
www.muji.co.uk Great transparent products so you can see what you've stored.
www.bpca.org.uk British Pest Control Association if you have a serious moth infestation.

Simple living

www.buynothingday.co.uk Once a year give your wallet a rest.
www.simpleliving.net offers-tips on how to unclutter your life.

RECOMMENDED READING

Here are some of my favourite books on clutter and related topics.

Don Aslett, *Clutter Free! Finally and Forever*, Betterway Books, 1995
Rita Emmett, *The Procrastinator's Handbook*, Walker Publishing, 2000
Sandra Felton, *The New Messies' Manual*, Revell, 2000
John F. Freyer, *All My Life for Sale*, Bloomsbury Publishing, 2002
Polly Ghazi and Judy Jones, *Downshifting*, Hodder & Stoughton, 2004
Cindy Glovinsky, *Making Peace with the Things in Your Life*, St Martin's Press, 2002
Alvin Hall, *Your Money or Your Life*, Coronet, 2002

Clutter-free forever

Karen Kingston, *Clear Your Clutter with Feng Shui*, Piatkus, 1998

Janet Luhrs, *The Simple Living Guide*, Broadway Books, 1997

Ann Maurice, *House Doctor Quick Fixes*, HarperCollins, 2001

Juliet Schor, *The Overspent American (Why we want what we don't need)*, HarperCollins, 1998

Kim Woodburn and Aggie MacKenzie, *How Clean Is Your House?*, Michael Joseph, 2003